JUST WHEN DID

Spiritual Gifts

CEASE?

Dʀ. Rɪᴄᴋʏ Rᴏʙᴇʀᴛs

CREATION
HOUSE PRESS
A Sᴛʀᴀɴɢ Cᴏᴍᴘᴀɴʏ

JUST WHEN DID SPIRITUAL GIFTS CEASE?
by Dr. Ricky Roberts
Published by Creation House Press
A Strang Company
600 Rinehart Road
Lake Mary, FL 32746
www.creationhouse.com

Unless otherwise noted, the Scripture quotations are from the King James Version of the Bible.

Scripture quotations marked NKJV are from the New King James Version of the Bible. Copyright © 1979, 1980, 1982 by Thomas Nelson, Inc., publishers. Used by permission.

Cover design by Kirk Douponce,
www.udgdesignworks.com
Interior design by David Bilby

Library of Congress Control Number: 2003105732
International Standard Book Number: 1-59185-235-8

This book was previously published by Dr. Ricky Roberts, ISBN 0-8187-0339-3, copyright © 2000.

03 04 05 06 — 8 7 6 5 4 3 2 1

Printed in the United States of America

*To all those who still believe in the
God of the miraculous.*

CONTENTS

INTRODUCTION

Every century, it seems that the Holy Spirit manifests His power through His gifts of anointing, healing and miracles to a sinful and depraved world. As long as God endures, the Holy Spirit works to perform these manifestations. The Holy Spirit was the banner of the early church and the foundation of their dogma.

The history of the church is also filled with evidence of the manifestations of the Holy Spirit. If we remove references to these works of power, church history is not only incomplete, but it is also lifeless. History proves that these manifestations were not counterfeit as some people may imagine. Those who experienced these works of power were truly of God. Without these supernatural manifestations of the Holy Spirit, Christianity is nothing more than a dead religion and a futile hope. One of the things that distinguishes Christianity from theism is the miraculous.

Saint Paul himself said that it was through mighty signs and wonders and by the power of the Spirit of God that the gospel of Christ was fulfilled in his ministry. (See Romans 15:19.) The gospel cannot be realized without the manifestations of the Holy Spirit. No wonder the early church said that the gospel of the Apostles was truly full and that they taught the "full gospel." The failure of the church today is due in large part to its rejection of the Holy Spirit, His gifts and their manifestation within the church. Many in the modern church give no place to the Holy Spirit. This grieves the Spirit of God who yearns for a place within His church where He can manifest His power to a dying world.

The purpose of the cross is redemption. The intention of Pentecost is to give the church power from on high. I believe that the church has failed to convert warlocks, witches, Satanists and other occultists because the purpose of Pentecost is not being manifested. Those who are involved in the occult do not respect the Word of God, but they do respect true power. The Holy Spirit works upon them, not by His Word at first, but through mighty signs of His power. I have seen occultists run to the altar and accept the Lord after seeing the power of the Holy Spirit up close.

Miracles and healing are the bread of the saints. (See Matthew 15:26.) They are indications that God is alive and well upon this planet and that the Word of God has been and is continuing to be sustained, substantiated and proven. Miraculous manifestations of the Spirit bring freedom to all those who are oppressed because the Lord is there and working before the people. (See Isaiah 61:1.) Did not Paul himself say, "Where the Spirit of the Lord is, there is liberty" (2 Cor. 3:17)? The Holy Spirit brings this liberation through His supernatural manifestations.

This book's premise is that the Holy Spirit and His gifts are alive and moving upon the earth and must still have a place within God's church. This is based upon scriptural and historical evidence and is a witness that in the craziness of the world, healing and miracles are still performed by God. It is a vindication that our God lives.

While the purpose of this work is to give proof that the Holy Spirit presently continues to perform miracles, healing, deliverance and other manifestations, this work does not approve of or promote the fanaticism and hysteria that are sometimes found in neo-Pentecostal circles. Fanaticism and hysteria have never saved, healed or delivered anyone for Christ. On the contrary, they bring confusion, embarrassment and shame upon the cause of Christ. It is an emotionalism wrought in the midst of psychological exercise or release. It is not godly, nor does it represent the holiness of God, His greatness or His majesty. This kind of fanatical Christian is not surrendering himself to the direction, supervision, influence and power of the Holy Spirit. Rather, he or she is surrendering to being out of control, following the beat of the music and the hysteria of the moment.

The river of the Holy Spirit flows in many ways and directions, yet the river has banks. These boundaries define what is of God and what is not of Him in accordance with God's written Word. (See 1 John 5:5–10.) Today it seems common for there to be no apparent limits in some neo-Pentecostal circles. There is often an open and endless river of pure hysteria and fanaticism, which is of the flesh. This ongoing emotionalism is not centered on Jesus Christ, the Bible or the cross. Without these three guides at our center, we have no precise directional flow for the river.

Several unbiblical manifestations have been described as occurring within these circles. I can find no scriptural authority for the following:

☦ After appearing to experience some ungodly type of "being slain in the Spirit," some people completely stripped off their clothing and were naked.

☦ Some, after the same manifestation, exhibited lewd behavior within the church.

☦ Some barked and howled during the church meetings. The ancient revivalists believed that demons, not the Holy Spirit, barked like dogs from within a possessed person.

☦ Some who were barking and howling were commanded to stop by invoking the power of the blood. If these acts were genuine, there would have been no need to invoke the blood of Jesus. It is at His name, by the power of His blood, through the power of the cross and by the power of the Word that all things are done within the church through the Holy Spirit.

☦ During these meetings some were caught up in such a frenzy of ungodliness that special police patrols had to be used to keep down lascivious activities.

☦ People within these groups seem to be less concerned with testing the manifestations and where they come from, placing more emphasis instead on the outpourings themselves.

☦ Some dived into the air and were caught by others, believing that they were somehow set free from demons.

In chapter 3, I will address this subject in much greater depth. This particular chapter deals with how the outpouring of the Holy Spirit affects a person physically. I will attempt to prove that being slain in the Spirit, trembling and quaking and other physical manifestations can also be signs of the Holy Spirit's presence. However, it warns that these same physical effects may also be counterfeited. For this reason, the tests of Jonathan Edwards are given to help the reader separate what is genuine from what is counterfeit.

The Pentecostals of yesterday recognized that the Holy Spirit acted only in accordance with the authority of the Bible. This is in keeping with 1 John 5:5–10, which demands that the Spirit and the Word must agree. Even more than that, the Word must temper the Spirit and the Spirit the Word. Experience must be judged by the Word, rather than the Word being judged by experience. By not following scriptural guidelines, we run the risk of accepting counterfeit supernatural manifestations rather than the genuine article. We need to search the Scriptures as commanded in Acts 17:10–11!

I acknowledge that there are many genuine manifestations of the Holy Spirit today. But there are also many that appear to be deceptive, destroying that which is genuine by discrediting such manifestations.

As the reader will discover, I am a firm believer in the manifestations of the Holy Spirit. I follow the ancient path set down by the early church. I base my views upon Greek grammar in particular, as well as the Revivalists and the views of the early church. The outlook of the early church was Pentecostal in its view of the Spirit and His works, but they also recognized that genuine and counterfeit manifestations always reside together.

It seems that as long as sin abounds, genuine and counterfeit manifestations will appear together. Christians should be careful not to reject the genuine because of the counterfeit. By doing so, we grieve the Holy Spirit and do Him an injustice. We must pray to follow God's Word so closely that we can unequivocally enjoy the genuine outpouring of His Holy Spirit!

VERBUM IPSE DEUS

NOTES ON BIBLICAL TEXTS

All critical editions of the Greek New Testament were consulted in regards to the New Testament and its doctrine on the gift of tongues and other gifts of the Holy Spirit. Both the critical and majority views were considered. I refer to it as the Greek New Testament or the Greek text. The Hebrew text, known as the Masoretic text, was the reference for the material dealing with the Old Testament. The Septuagint, a translation of the uncorrupted Hebrew text, was also consulted in research on the Old Testament. In this book it will be referred to as the Greek Septuagint.

PRONUNCIATION NOTES

I have used the Modern Greek pronunciation in this book rather than that derived from Erasmus. Modern Greek pronunciation more closely resembles that of Ancient Greek than the manner in which Erasmus pronounced Greek. Byzantine scholars pronounced Ancient and Modern Greek in the same manner. Even before the close of the first century, the pronunciation of Ancient Greek is replicated in the Modern Greek. In the fifteenth century, the Greeks still pronounced the Greek language as Plato, Euripides and Aristophanes did. Furthermore, papyri refute the Erasmian pronunciation. The vowels and diphthongs, coming from the Alexandrine period and written in Koine Greek, were not pronounced in the same manner as those found in the pronunciation of Erasmus, but in the same manner as found in modern Greek.

The pronunciation of Hebrew used in this book is commonly used throughout colleges that still teach Hebrew. It is almost universally considered to be the closest to the pronunciation of Ancient Hebrew.

Transliterations follow the text to help you pronounce the various Hebrew and Greek words presented.

CHAPTER ONE

Scriptural Evidence for the Gifts

Individuals often use Scripture to give weight to their own opinions that may not be founded upon biblical principles of interpretation. This is sometimes the approach used to deny the existence and use of spiritual gifts. Scripture is referred to as their source and foundation, but it is really tradition and misinterpretation that are the basis of their thought and opinion. Examining relevant Scripture and Greek grammar reveal that the gifts of the Spirit and their manifestations are alive and well.

I like to use the phrase, "a God who does not work is no God at all." Those who deny the continuation of supernatural gifts almost always base their beliefs on nothing more than tradition. Others deny the manifestations of the Holy Spirit simply because they haven't seen them in action. There is not one scripture that even hints at the notion that supernatural gifts ceased at the time of the apostles. What would happen if a new convert were given a Bible and told to go into a room and study the New Testament from beginning to end? I believe that at the end of that time, the new believer would come out of the room believing in healings, miracles and all nine supernatural gifts of the Holy Spirit.

I am a firm believer in *sola Scriptura*, which means "Scripture alone." On the other hand, I am also a firm believer in the Holy Spirit and His workings. There must be a balance between the two. The following sections are written to keep that equilibrium in check and to show that there is no proof that the gifts have ceased.

GIFTS ARE NOT TEMPORARY

The nine supernatural gifts mentioned in chapters 12 and 14 of 1 Corinthians are not viewed anywhere in Scripture as temporary with other gifts being considered permanent. The term *temporary* means that these gifts were given only for the apostolic age and soon afterward ceased. It is the belief that the spiritual gifts of the Holy Spirit and their manifestations were temporary and soon ceased to be a part of the ministry of the Holy Spirit.

The nine supernatural gifts mentioned in these chapters of 1 Corinthians are the word of wisdom, the word of knowledge, the gift of faith, the gifts of healing, the working of miracles, the gift of prophecy, the gift of discerning of spirits, the gift of tongues and the gift of interpretation of tongues.

If these nine gifts of the Spirit are temporary, then by the same logic, all gifts, including salvation, sanctification and justification, would also be temporary. This would also include gifts that are considered "permanent." These are the gifts of teaching, helping, administration, evangelism, pastoring, exhortation, giving and showing mercy. (See Romans 12:7–8; 1 Corinthians 12:28; Ephesians 4:11; 12:8–10.) Should we also then conclude that the fruits of the Spirit were only temporary and that all aspects of God are nothing more than an illusion? God forbid!

PERFECTION IS TO COME

Paul writes in 1 Corinthians 13:10, "But when that which is perfect is come, then that which is in part will be done away." Many use this to prove that the supernatural gifts of the Holy Spirit ceased at the end of the apostolic age.

This part of Corinthians does not deal with the end of the apostolic age at all. The Greek text clearly reveals that the whole verse is dealing with the eternal perfect state. This faultless condition takes place when the partial is done away with, when the heavens and the earth are reborn after the millennium and the last rebellion, and the Great White Throne is established. Since partial knowledge continues to exist today, tongues and the rest of the gifts of the Holy Spirit must still be available. (See 1 Corinthians 13:8–10.) There will be a probability that the gifts will be withdrawn only when partial knowledge ceases. In verse eight, partial knowledge, prophecy and tongues are seen at the beginning of the perfect state to be absolutely abolished.

By using the *subjunctive mood*, the passage literally means that at the arrival of the perfect state there is a possibility that some supernatural gifts of the Holy Spirit may still be in use. (See Revelation 21.) Accordingly, the use of other gifts may be extended. God did not unequivocally reveal to Paul the absolute certainty that all the gifts would end at that time. We do not definitely know either way whether all the gifts will end at this time or whether some will continue. God is the only One who knows and it is His decision alone.

"But when perfection, or the perfect state, will probably come instantaneously, then that which is in part will be abolished." This is probably the best translation of 1 Corinthians 13:10. The idea of the Greek adjective τέλειος (tĕlēōs) is far more powerful in thought than many understand. It expresses complete and utter perfection. It is all-inclusive and refers to such a flawless state that it cannot be described by what occurs at the Rapture, the Resurrection, the Second Advent, the completion of the New Testament canon, the maturity of the church or the millennium. All these things show incompleteness and imperfection because sin and bondage continue. The state of perfection will only exist when sin and bondage are abolished.

This same Greek adjective is used in the *neuter gender*. This eliminates Christ from being the perfection referred to here. Then it means the perfect state that occurs after the Millennium. The very use of the *neuter gender* demands that this Greek adjective must be translated "perfection." This is a future and eternal state of achievement for creation, without sin and evil, that has yet to take place.

Paul's uncertainty about the time element for the cessation of the gifts and whether they would even cease is clear. The apostle only states that they may cease at the time of the perfect state. (See Revelation 21.) He even concludes that God may allow some to continue. The use of the *subjunctive mood* indicates that the only time there will be even a chance for the gifts to end is at the perfect state. Before that time, Paul uses the *subjunctive mood* to stress the impossibility of the gifts ceasing.

The Greek adverb τότε (tōtĕ) shows that what is referred to is the future state. It denotes a time to come, which will be the eternal state. Expressions such as, "But when perfection will probably come," "We shall see face to face," and "I shall know fully, even as I am fully known," all deal with the perfect state referred to in this passage. (See 1 Corinthians 12:8–12.) Revelation 22:4 also states that at this future time people will see His face, in completeness and perfection.

Early church fathers Archelaus, the bishop of Chaschar, and Origen, a biblical critic and theologian, agree with this interpretation.[1] Indeed, Origen connects both the expression, "face to face" and the expression "But when perfection will probably come" with the renovation of the heavens and the earth. This was the most dominant view at the time. Methodius, who was bishop of Lycia, held the only other notable view. He believed that the perfection mentioned here would occur at the appearance of the millennial kingdom.[2] The view that perfection would rise at the end of the apostolic age, (100 A.D.) when the church reached maturity and the New Testament canon was completed, cannot be defended either from the Scriptures or from the early church fathers.

The Greek verb παύω (pävō) means "to cease" or "to stop." It is connected to the gift of tongues in 1 Corinthians 13. In this instance, it is used in the *middle voice*. This is very important because the middle voice points to the fact that tongues will cease in and of themselves. God does not directly have to cause them to cease. Paul's focus is only on the gift of tongues forthright. Yet, he identifies that all communication by speech will cease. When? With the arrival of that perfection, all creation will no longer need an imperfect means of communicating. Since imperfection will give way to perfection, tongues will end because their purpose is completed. Languages remain in use until the perfect comes because of the rebellion by mankind and Satan. When perfection comes, written or spoken language will no longer be needed. Communication will be accomplished through the mind and the thoughts of the mind. This will be God's perfect means of communication. This type of communication cannot be duplicated. Our communication today, even God speaking through thoughts and minds, is imperfect due to sin. Sin must be removed before perfect communication can be experienced in creation. Until perfection comes, even the resurrected saints will not be able to communicate with God in this perfect manner.

Tertullian, a third-century father of the early church, stated that the sciences would also cease along with tongues and prophecies.[3] He equated the continuation of the sciences with the continued use of tongues and prophecies.

In 1 Corinthians 13:8, the Greek verb παύω (pävō) is expressed in the *momentary future tense.* The very use of this tense gives strong evidence that the gifts of tongues and prophecy will be abolished instantaneously as a means of communicating God's will to men. As long as man speaks, the gift of tongues will continue. Where there is partial knowledge, there will be prophecies and tongues. Therefore, prophecies, tongues and partial knowledge must come to an end so that God can bring forth a perfect knowledge and a perfect means of communication. Paul tells his readers that prophecies will be abolished and tongues will cease. The Greek verb καταργέω (kätäryĕō) means "to render useless, powerless, unmeaning, to annihilate, or to abolish." Paul sets forth that both prophecies and tongues will have a definite ending, one that is gradual but complete and permanent. He does not say that they will end for a time and then reappear, but he means that when they do end, they will end for good.

The absence of the article before prophesies and tongues in the Greek is a strong indication of this view. Paul refers to partial knowledge, prophecies and tongues

as childish things that will be done away with when perfection comes. He is letting us know that there is a time
coming when prophecies will no longer be used as a
means of communicating God's will to people. Prophecy is
limited and can only impart a partial knowledge of God's
will and plan. This future tense of the verb shows that
these gifts will still be in use and will end in an abrupt
instant. The verb is stated in the passive voice, showing
that at the time of perfection, prophecy, as a means of
communicating with men, will end. With the ushering in
of the perfect state, perfect communication between God
and man will begin.

GIFTS NOT LIMITED TO THREE HISTORICAL PERIODS

Cessationists argue that supernatural manifestations are
limited to three periods of biblical history. According to
this theory, the three periods took place in the days of
Moses and Joshua, during the ministries of Elijah and
Elisha, and at the time of Christ and the apostles. Each
period lasted only two generations long.

The major problems with this belief are:

- ✝ Because the Holy Spirit is still working, His gifts
  will continue to be manifest until the time of the
  perfect state. In the perfect state, there is only a
  probability that all of them will be done away
  with and a possibility that some will continue.
- ✝ Speech, writing and partial knowledge have not
  ceased. Until these cease, tongues and prophecies will not end, nor is it likely that other gifts
  will cease.
- ✝ There is no stated biblical purpose for the three
  alleged periods of miracles.
- ✝ Jeremiah, according to the Masoretic Hebrew
  text, states categorically that signs and wonders
  were even occurring in his own time both in
  Israel and in other nations. This was after the
  period of Elijah and Elisha and before the period
  of Christ and the apostles. (See Jeremiah 32:20.)

- ☩ Samuel introduced the age of the prophets, not Elijah. (See 1 Samuel 3:19–21.)
- ☩ Before Samuel, groups of prophets were already being used by the Holy Spirit. (See Samuel 10:5.)
- ☩ The apostles did not write all the books of the New Testament. Luke, Mark and Jude were not apostles, yet they testified that signs and wonders were present among all the believers.
- ☩ Not all those that accomplished signs and wonders in the times of the apostles were themselves apostles. (See Acts 1:10–11; 2; 6:8; 8:6–13, 18; 9:10–18; 10:45–46; 11:28; 13:1; 14:4–14; 15:32; 19:6; 21:4, 9.)
- ☩ There are too many miracles and other manifestations of the supernatural outside of this time frame to make this belief defensible.[4]

Outside of these three limited periods of miracles, there are many other manifestations of supernatural gifts: 1) appearances by the Lord, as well as angels, to people, 2) evidence of supernatural deliverance and rescue by God or His angels, 3) supernatural empowering of strength and prophecy, 4) supernatural judgments, 5) supernatural dreams, visions and trances, 6) supernatural interpretation of dreams and visions, 7) supernatural healings and ideas, 8) signs and wonders, 9) a consistent prophetic ministry from the time of Samuel until the end of the Old Testament canon.

By means of the Holy Spirit, the Old Testament saints were endowed with all the nine gifts of the Spirit, except the gift of tongues and the gift of interpretation of tongues.

GIFTS OF SPIRIT STILL GIVEN

In 1 Corinthians 12:7–10, the Greek verb δίδωμι (thēthōmē), found in the Greek text, is in the *present tense*. Like the future tense, the *present tense* has several meanings. In this particular case, the type of the *present tense* used is known as the *customary present*. This tense represents action that occurs repeatedly on a regular basis. Paul recognizes two major things about the manifestations of the Holy Spirit in reference to the customary present. He expects the manifestations of the Holy Spirit as evidenced by these gifts to be easily seen and experienced. These manifestations are expected to be repeated throughout every age until that perfection of age comes when some manifestations may continue.

STRIVE AFTER THE GIFTS

The Holy Spirit declared through Paul in 1 Corinthians 12:31, "But you strive after the better spiritual gifts always." If the gifts would be done away with, why would Paul state this? In this passage the Holy Spirit is commanding the saints to strive after all of His gifts. If the Holy Spirit knew that the gifts were going to cease at the end of the apostolic age, why would He use Paul to encourage the saints to strive after these better spiritual gifts? There is a passion for desiring the gifts that is conveyed in this passage.

The Greek word for "you strive always" is ζηλοῦτε (zēloutĕ). Apostle Paul is using the *imperative*. In this instance it is known as the *imperative of command*. In essence, Paul is commanding that all the saints strive for and earnestly desire the supernatural gifts of the Holy Spirit. Paul directs the saints to hunger for the gifts so that they are equipped with power to fight Satan and are assisted in their walk and growth with Christ in accordance with the Word of God. How can that command be fulfilled today if the supernatural gifts have ended? Was Paul wrong? On the other hand, was the Holy Spirit wrong for inspiring Paul to write this?

DO NOT DESPISE PROPHECY

Paul warns the Christians at Thessalonica not to hate or despise prophesying. (See 1 Thessalonians 5:20.) Apparently some within this church despised the use of the supernatural gifts. Paul strongly warns them against doing this. Literally, the Greek text is translated, "You hate not prophecies." The Greek verb ἐξουθενέω (ĕxouthĕvĕō) is translated "despise" or "hate," and may also mean "to

SCRIPTURAL EVIDENCE FOR THE GIFTS 9

make light of" or even "to condemn." This verb is used in the *imperative mood* and in particular the *imperative of negative command*. The Thessalonians appeared to despise prophecy because it was easily abused. This does not cancel out genuine prophecy or its rightful interpretation. In simple terms, Paul is saying that prophecy is worth all the shortcomings that may come along with it.

The Thessalonians decided to reject all prophecy of any kind just to be on the safe side. Paul recognized that dismissing all prophecy because of wrong interpretations or misuse, was a travesty.

The misinterpretation of prophecy that occurred in the life of Paul can be attributed to others. In one case, Paul states that he has already been bound by the Holy Spirit to go to Jerusalem. (See Acts 20:22; 24:17; Romans 15:2.) Others, "through the Spirit," said that he should not go. (See Acts 20:33; 21:4, 10–11.) How does one interpret this contradiction? The answer rests not upon what the Holy Spirit told Paul at all, but upon how the others interpreted what God spoke to them.

Paul was convinced that his decision to go to Jerusalem was of the Holy Spirit. The disciples, mentioned in Acts 21:4, had been told by the Spirit what would befall Paul should he go there. They interpreted this warning of danger as a command for Paul not to go to Jerusalem. The word of prophecy was correct, but their interpretation of it was not. It was a warning of what Paul would face by going to Jerusalem. In Acts 21:33, the prophecy by Agabus was indeed of God, but was a description of the dangers that Paul would face at Jerusalem. Agabus never said that Paul should not go to Jerusalem even though others begged him not to go.

These two examples of prophecy were intended to help Paul realize the dangers of going to Jerusalem. The Holy Spirit did not forbid him to go but was unmistakably warning him of the dangers that would befall him. This is the reason that Paul said that he was ready for the sake of Christ not only to be bound, but also to die!

The gift of prophecy in the New Testament is shown as

not being equal to the authority of Scripture. (See Acts 21:3, 10–11; 1 Thessalonians 5:19–21; 1 Corinthians 14:29–38.) This is true also for the other eight spiritual gifts of the Holy Spirit. The purpose of the gifts is not to supercede or even to equal the Word of God, but to confirm it.

In other words, the common view that the gifts of the Spirit are of equal authority to the Scripture is inconsistent with their use before the completion of the New Testament and after the closing of the Old Testament. Notice that even before the completion of the New Testament, the early church sought after the scriptures of the Old Testament to support doctrine and settle disputes, rather than rest upon New Testament prophets. (See Acts 2:16; 15:15; 26:22.)

THE GIFTS ARE THE CHANNEL OF GOD'S POWER

Without the supernatural gifts a person can possess a false form of godliness while denying the power of real godliness as recorded in 2 Timothy 3:5. A person who only pretends to be living a holy Christian life exhibits this false form of godliness. Such a person is a Christian in name only, not in fact or substance; he is saved, but weak in faith, having no heavenly power and authority.

The Greek noun for power is δύναμις (thēnämēs). This power is manifested through the supernatural gifts of the Spirit. This same Greek noun describes the power that Jesus had through the Holy Spirit to heal sickness and to cast out demons. (See Mark 3:15; Luke 4:36.) This is the same authority that Jesus gave to His disciples. (See Mark 6:7; Luke 9:1.) This same power is received at the baptism of the Holy Spirit, and it is the same power that enabled Stephen to perform great and mighty signs and wonders (See Acts 1:8; 6:8.)

To the apostle Paul, the Holy Spirit's power is manifested through the supernatural gifts of the Holy Spirit. If the means of manifesting God's power are taken away, one must also reject the continuation of God's power. This manifestation of God's power through the supernatural gifts will mostly end at the dawn of the perfect state. Even if certain gifts continue to be used for a time in the perfect state, the power of God will not need to be manifested through the gifts of the Holy Spirit because His power will encompass and possess all things. In other words, until the perfect state, the gifts are the very channel through which God's power flows. Once perfection is achieved, the power of God will flow directly throughout all of creation.

While the characteristics Paul gives to describe the last days deal primarily with apostates, genuine Christians may even take upon themselves some of these End-Time tendencies without becoming apostate. (See 2 Timothy 3:2–9.) Some Christians may deny the continuation of the supernatural gifts or the continuation of the power of God manifested through these gifts and still not be considered apostate.

Moreover, according to Paul, the power that is manifested through the supernatural gifts of the Spirit is the power that must be delivered with the gospel, lest it become dead. (See 1 Thessalonians 1:5.) The Word of God, when spoken, is lifeless without the power of God manifested through the supernatural gifts of the Spirit.

Furthermore, the definition of Christ's gospel, given by Paul in Romans 1:16, is very remarkable. According to Greek thought, Paul defines the gospel as the power of God that is channeled through the supernatural gifts of the Holy Spirit for the purpose of salvation. If the supernatural gifts are no longer in use then the channel by which God's power can flow is abolished. If the channel is removed, then all the saints who were supposedly saved after the first century were saved in appearance only. God forbid! Therefore this channel, through which the gifts of the Holy Spirit and their manifestations flow, must still exist today!

This channel does not have to be outwardly manifested within a church service for the power to flow into it. All that is needed for the Holy Spirit's power to flow in a church service is the belief of one person in these gifts. God can perform healings and miracles based upon faith alone, without using anyone as a vehicle to manifest His power, but the gifts of the Holy Spirit will remain in the background. These gifts are the channel of God's power and the only means whereby His power can flow so that a person can be healed or miracles wrought. The appearance of healings and miracles commonly take place when a saint of God, equipped with these gifts, is used by God as a vehicle to manifest them.

John 7:39 indicates that the Holy Spirit had not yet been given to the apostles and to the church. How then did the apostles, the seventy disciples, and the rest of the church do such signs and miracles before the Holy Spirit was given? The power did not come directly from the Holy Spirit, but through Christ. That power, through Christ, was manifested in the gifts until the coming of the Holy Spirit. When the Holy Spirit was given, the apostles, disciples and the church were able to use all of the gifts. Before the giving of the Spirit, the apostles and the rest did mighty works through the power manifested in the gifts that came from Christ. The Holy Spirit rested only upon Christ at this time. Consequently, He was the only One endowed with the gifts.

THE PROPHET JOEL AND THE GIFTS

Joel 2:28–29 indicates that after the restoration of Israel and before the millennium, the Holy Spirit will be poured out again. Prophecies, dreams and visions will be given until the millennium ends. The key words that show this are "restore" in verse 25 and "afterward" in verse 28. Using the Greek Septuagint and the Masoretic Hebrew texts, verse 28 has four literal meanings: 1) the pouring out of the Holy Spirit at Pentecost and the manifestation of prophecies, dreams and visions afterward, 2) the pouring out of the Holy Spirit from time to time after Pentecost and the manifestation of prophecies, dreams and visions from time to time after Pentecost, 3) the pouring out of the Holy Spirit after the Rapture and the manifestation of prophecies, dreams and visions caused by God after the Rapture, 4) the pouring out of the Holy Spirit after the tribulation will be going on during the millennium. The manifestations of prophecies, dreams and visions caused by God after the tribulation will also be ongoing throughout the millennium.

The events in this passage were partially fulfilled at Pentecost and have continued to come to fruition over the centuries. They will only be completely fulfilled from the time of the tribulation to the end of the millennium. Hence, the spiritual gifts have not ended as some suppose.

FALSE ASSUMPTIONS ABOUT THE GIFTS

Many times people make false assumptions about the supernatural gifts. For example, many believe that healing during the times of Jesus and the apostles was always automatic. *Automatic* literally means that Christ and His apostles could heal anyone, at anytime, anywhere at will. This is not what the Scriptures teach. Luke 5:17, John 5:1–6, and Mark 6:5–6 all prove that there were limitations placed upon the gifts of healing. Neither Christ nor the apostles could use the gifts of healing anytime, anywhere they wanted.

If the gifts of the Holy Spirit were limited in how they were used in Christ's life, then it must be true for anyone who has been endowed with any supernatural gift. The gifts are the gifts of the Holy Spirit, not the gifts of men.

These same doubters see the early church as totally absent of all sickness and disease. But this is not the case. Sickness and disease occurred in the early church, like they do in the modern church. (See Philippians 2:27; 2 Timothy 4:20; James 5:14–16; 1 Corinthians 11:30.) They were not completely eradicated from the early church by the supernatural power of God. Rather, it was a constant struggle. In some cases, sickness and disease were a direct result of sin and were initiated by God as a judgment against disobedience. (See 1 Corinthians 11:30.)

Consequently, in the early church physical healing was contingent, not universal. Not every person that the apostles themselves prayed for was healed. This taught the apostles that God was the Master, not the servant, and could not be manipulated.

Many see, in Christ's ministry, the total accomplishment of healing in whomever Christ prayed to receive wholeness. Yet, the English translations do injustice to the original thought in such passages. (See Matthew 10:1; 4:23–24; 8:16; 12:15; Luke 6:19; Acts 10:38.) In these passages, the Greek thought is that although many whom Christ prayed for were healed, not all were. The Greek adjective πᾶς (päs) does not have the article before it. When this Greek adjective does not have the article before it, it can only mean "a considerable amount." Written in this way, the adjective indicates that not everyone that wanted healing at the time that Christ prayed for them received it. It is still the task of the saints to pray for healing, regardless of the outcome.

Remember that Christ only saw a very few people healed in Nazareth. (See Mark 6:5.) From this verse, there seems to have been a limitation of the gifts of healing in Christ's ministry at Nazareth. Why? Primarily this is because of doubt on the part of the sick individual. This also reveals that not everyone Christ or the apostles prayed for was healed.

Healing confirmed by Christ and reinstituted in the New Testament has limits.[5] These limitations are due to the very fact that healing is found within a covenant. This covenant is known as the "healing covenant." This was at first found in the Old Testament and later transferred to the New Testament by Christ's death on the cross. (See Exodus 15:26; Isaiah 53; Matthew 8:17; 1 Peter 2:24.)

Exodus 15:26 is the very passage upon which the "healing covenant" is founded. This passage reads:

> And said, If thou wilt diligently hearken to the voice of the Lord thy God, and wilt do that which is right in his sight, and wilt give ear to his commandments, and keep all his statutes, I will put none of these diseases upon thee, which I have brought upon the Egyptians: for I *am* the Lord that healeth thee.

There are three promises in the healing covenant that have been brought over into the New Testament.

✟ God will not put sickness and disease upon an
    obedient person unless it is for testing. (See
    Exodus 15:26; Revelation 22:18–19.)
✟ God is the one who heals. (See Exodus 15:26;
    Isaiah 53:5; 1 Peter 2:24.)
✟ God will take away one's sickness when their
    test is over or when their disobedience is over.
    (See Exodus 23:25.)

The healing covenant places strong conditions on
healing from the Almighty. (See Exodus 15:26.) Indeed,
the healing covenant strongly advocates that God is the
One who can heal. Yet, if a person sins, He is also the One
who can take away His healing and put back the sickness
as judgment upon that person. As such, God heals on His
own terms and not on the terms of man. In order to
receive healing from God a person must meet God's
terms. This is also true for keeping a healing.

Exodus 15:26, Isaiah 53:5 and 1 Peter 2:24 clarify God's
position as it relates to healing as found in the healing
covenant. It is God's will and desire to heal all. Therefore,
from God's perspective, healing is unconditional and
unconditionally desired to be given to all. On the other
hand, in James 5:16 and 3 John 1:2, the *subjunctive mood* is
used giving the conditions for the healing. For man then,
healing is always conditional and depends upon all the
conditions being met and in agreement with each other.
James and John understood divine healing to mean that a
saint will probably receive healing when he asks. It is our
responsibility to do all that we can to receive our healing.
It is God's responsibility to make sure that if all these things
are in agreement, then healing can take place. There are
seven noted conditions of the healing covenant.

1. Time. (See Jeremiah 14:18–19; Ecclesiastes 3:3.)

2. Faith. (See Matthew 9:21–22; James 5:14–15; 1
   Corinthians 11:27–32; 1 Peter 2:24; Matthew
   8:16–17.)

3. Will of God. (See 1 John 5:14.)

4. Obedience. (See Exodus 15:26; Leviticus 26:3,
   14–26; Jeremiah 14:18–22.)

5. Will of man. (See Romans 7; Daniel 8:4; Luke 24:51; Deuteronomy 30:15; John 7:17; Hebrews 3:5, 7–8; 4:7; John 1:12–13.)

6. Partial grace. (See Exodus 33:19.)

7. The ending of judgment or testing.[6]

HINDRANCES TO HEALING

✝ Wrong motive. (See James 4:23.)

✝ Doubt. (See Matthew 11:23–24.)

✝ Praying against God's will. (See 1 John 5:14.)

✝ Iniquity in the heart. (See Psalm 66:18.)

✝ Refusal to hear God's law. (See Proverbs 28:9.)

✝ An estranged heart. (See Isaiah 29:13.)

✝ Sinful separation from God. (See Isaiah 59:2.)

✝ Waywardness. (Jeremiah 14:10–12.)

✝ Offering unworthy sacrifices. (See Malachi 1:7–9.)

✝ Praying to be seen of men. (See Matthew 6:5.)

✝ Pride in fasting and tithing. (See Luke 18:11–14.)

✝ Lack of faith. (See Hebrews 11:6.)

✝ Asking wrongly to spend it on selfish passions. (See James 4:3.)

✝ Inconsideration of husband or wife. (See 1 Peter. 3:7.)

✝ Lack of understanding the Word of God. (See Hosea 4:6; 2 Corinthians 5:17.)

✝ Lack of understanding what a new creation is. (See 2 Corinthians 5:17.)

✝ Lack of understanding one's place in Christ. (See 1 John 4:4.)

✝ Lack of understanding righteousness. (See James 5:16.)

✝ Lack of understanding our right to use the name of Jesus. (See Acts 2:38; 3:6; 4:18; 5:40; 9:27; 16:18.)

✝ Lack of not acting upon the Word. (See Matthew 4.)

✝ The stealing of the healing by Satan. (See John 10:10.)

✝ The person not being thankful or not giving testimonies about the healing. (See Luke 17:11–17; Ephesians 4:17; 3 John 1:3.)

HOW TO RECEIVE AND KEEP A HEALING

✝ Remain and continue in Christ Jesus. (See 1 John 2:24–25.)

✝ Remain and continue in the Word of the Lord. (See John 8:31.)

✝ Continue in the love of the Lord. (See John 15:9.)

✝ Continue in the very grace of God. (See Acts 13:43.)

✝ Continue to be sold out to God, walk and live his faith. (See Acts 13:48; John 3:16.)

✝ Continue in the goodness of God. (See Romans 11:20–24.)

✝ Continue in the faith grounded and settled, and be not moved away from the hope of the gospel. (See Colossians 1:22; Titus 1:2; Romans 8:24–25; Acts 14:22.)

✝ Continue to look into the perfect law of liberty. (See James 1:25.)

✝ Keep the commandments of God. (See John 15:9–10.)

✝ Continue in prayer. (See Colossians 4:2.)

✝ Continue in the doctrine of the gospel. (See 1 Timothy 4:11–16.)

✝ Continue to reject unbelief. (See Romans 11:20–24.)

✝ Do not walk in the sins of the past life, living that life again. (See John 1:12; 1 John 5:1; Luke 8:13.)

✝ Persevere and endure all things for the prize of unconditional security and unconditional salvation. (See Mark 13:13; Matthew 24:13.)

✝ Live in the very state of obedience to holiness, grace and all that God stands for. (See 1 Peter 1:2; Acts 6:7; 2 Corinthians 6:9.)

✝ Do not commit any death penalty sin. (See Ezekiel 3:17–21; 18:4–29; Romans 1:21–32; 1

Corinthians 6:9–11; Galatians 5:19–21.)

✝ Do not be removed from Christ or fall away from grace. (See Galatians 1:6–8.)

✝ Do not provoke God to anger and tempt Him with utter contempt. (See 1 Corinthians 10:13; Hebrews 3:16.)

✝ Do not refuse to hear, obey and follow Christ. (See John 10:27–29.)

✝ Make things right when you commit sin. (See 1 John 1:9; 2:1–2; James 5:19–20.)

✝ Do not allow Satan to steal the healing. (See John 10:10.)

✝ Continue to be thankful and give testimonies about the healing. (See Luke 17:11–17; Ephesians 4:17; 3 John 1:3.)

The hindrances to healing are also hindrances to fulfilled prophecy, answered prayer, deliverance and miracles within the lives of the saints. How to keep and receive a healing is the same manner in how one keeps and receives a fulfilled prophecy, an answered prayer, deliverance and a miracle.

GRADUAL VS. INSTANTANEOUS HEALING

The healing covenant provides for both gradual healing and instantaneous, miraculous healing. A simple healing is one that is not done immediately, but is gradually accomplished. This is done to test the person receiving the healing to see if he will accept God's gift of wholeness and walk in it or whether he will turn back to sinful disobedience.

Though some deny that gradual healing is noted in Scripture, it can be found. For example, Naaman was gradually healed of leprosy. (See 2 Kings 5:10–14.) Every time he dipped himself into the Jordan River, he was partially healed. By the seventh segment, Naaman was completely healed. One must also not forget Hezekiah. (See 2 Kings 20:1–11.) He was not healed instantaneously. His complete recovery occurred on the third day. In John

4:50–52, the nobleman's son was healed gradually. The words "began to amend" establish this. In Mark 8:22–26, Christ had to pray for a blind man to receive his sight not once, but twice. The first time he received a partial healing. The second time he received a complete recovery.

The usage of the *linear* and *punctilliar* kinds of action in the Greek, Hebrew and Latin grammars attest to instantaneous healing and gradual healing. Often when a healing is referred to in a passage, it can be either one. When many healings are noted in a passage, it is implied by the grammar that in the midst of miraculous healings, there are also simple healings. For example, in Mark 16:18, Christ confesses that the sick "shall recover," but according to Greek grammar, the recovery may be instantaneous and immediate. On the other hand, it may be gradual, through several segments that may consist of minutes, hours, days, weeks, months or even years. In James 5:14–15, James agrees with what is noted in Mark 16:18. James confesses that "the prayer of faith shall save the sick, and the Lord shall raise him up." The phrases "shall save" and "shall raise" prove in Greek thought that on one occasion the healing is instantaneous and immediate while on the other occasion it is gradual.

GIFTS OF HEALING DID NOT END WITH PAUL

Some believe that the gifts of healing were already beginning to cease during Paul's ministry even before his death. They point to the examples of Epaphroditus, Trophimus and Timothy as firm proof of this. (See Philippians 2:25–27; 2 Timothy 4:20; 1 Timothy 5:23.) However, this is not an indication that the gifts of healing had ceased. Rather, it shows that God has a time and a place for healing people, and that in this instance, it was not the right time. God allowed this to occur to show Paul that He is the only One who performs the healing. Paul himself admitted that he had a problem with pride. (See 2

Corinthians 12:7.) Consequently, God did not automatically heal these brothers as a means of showing that it is only God who heals.

After Jesus had given the apostles power and authority over demons and diseases, the apostles themselves could not heal a demonized boy because of their lack of faith. (See Matthew 10:1; 17:16, 20; Luke 9:1.)

One must also remember that the supernatural gifts of the Holy Spirit were working in the lives of Epaphroditus, Trophimus and Timothy. Since each was not yet healed, it is apparent that the time and place for their healing had not yet occurred. It also indicates that no matter how many of the nine supernatural gifts God has bestowed upon a person, unless God wills, a healing cannot be done.

There is no proof that the supernatural gifts of the Spirit ceased with the death of the apostles. Stephen and Philip were given a ministry of signs and wonders similar to that of the apostles, even though they were not apostles. (See Acts 6:8; 8:6–13.)

Within each gift of the Spirit, there are degrees of power and strength. Because of this, the power of a gift within one person may be different from that in another person.

PURPOSES OF THE MIRACULOUS

Some have said that the only purpose of the miraculous was to authenticate the ministry of the apostles. The Bible does not support this view. The purpose of the miraculous is never mentioned in the Bible to be for authenticating the work of the apostles. The miraculous in the Word has several purposes.

- ✝ The miraculous is used to confirm the Word of God. (See Mark 16:20.)
- ✝ Miracles are used to bear witness to Jesus Christ and His Word. (See John 5:36.)
- ✝ The miraculous showed that Jesus was approved of God. (See Acts 2:22.)
- ✝ The miraculous is used to prove and to proclaim

the character of Jesus as Messiah and as God. (See John 3:2; 5:36; 9:32–33; Mark 2:10–11; Matthew 11:1–6; 12:28; 14:25–33.)

✝ The miraculous is used to authenticate the message and the Word about Jesus. (See Mark 16:20; Acts 14:3.)

Today signs, wonders, miracles and healings produce living signs and witnesses to the truth of the Word of God. These things establish and continue to emphasize the Scriptures as true and valid today. These are visible and tangible manifestations of God and proof that He is still dealing with mankind. They stress that He is not a dead god, but the only true and living God. They reveal that what He wrote, through the means of men, is the truth and the only way to learn about Him. They also prove that the Word of God reveals just how to be set free from sin and depravity and experience a state of grace and holiness.

The main purpose of the manifestations of the Holy Spirit today is to confirm and establish the Scripture as the only written Word of God. Before the completion of the written Word, their purpose was to testify and confirm the message within the books of the Old and New Testaments. Through all of these manifestations confirming, establishing, authenticating and testifying about the message written within the books, the books themselves were also confirmed, established, authenticated and testified about. The focus was more on the message rather than the books.

The need for these supernatural manifestations to confirm the ways of God is clearly seen in 1 Kings 18:21. Elijah confronts the prophets of Baal with God's power and authority. Miracles will always show the mighty hand of God in the midst of a wicked world.

Second Corinthians 12:12 is sometimes used as proof that miracles were done to provide authenticity to the message and apostleship of the apostles. But the Greek text refutes this. The text literally says, "The signs indeed of an apostle were performed among you in all, or much, endurance with signs, and wonders, and miracles." Paul indicates that he is a true apostle by his sufferings, life and ministry. (See 2 Corinthians 11:16–33; Galatians 6:17; 1 Corinthians 4:9–13; 2 Corinthians 6:3–10; 10–13.) If the purpose of the miraculous was to confirm and authenticate the apostles, why did those who were not apostles manifest the miraculous through their ministry?[7] Why did God give the gifts of healing, prophecy, faith, wisdom, the working of miracles and the other gifts to the church in particular if the miraculous was only intended to be used to confirm the apostleship of the apostles? (See 1 Corinthians 12:7–10; Galatians 3:5.) Miracles were not created to confirm apostleship. If the purpose of the miraculous was to confirm this, why did miracles, signs, wonders and healings accompany the ministry of Christ?

The signs that Paul mentions that prove that a person is an apostle cannot refer to miracles, healing or any such manifestation of the Holy Spirit. If Paul had meant for the proof of his apostleship to be the miraculous, he would have used the nominative case in Greek rather than the instrumental case in Greek. Signs, wonders and miracles are written in the grammatical construction known as the *instrumental of accompaniment*. This signifies that signs, wonders and miracles accompany the signs of an apostle. These signs are their sufferings, life and ministry. But it does not denote that the characteristics of an apostle are signs, wonders and miracles. If this were the case, then all who accomplished the miraculous would have been apostles, but according to the ministry of Stephen and Philip, this is not what the New Testament states. (See 1 Corinthians 12:7–10; Galatians 3:5.)

The writers never intended the miraculous to support their claims that they were writing Scripture. The authority of Scripture does not rest upon the miraculous manifestations of the Holy Spirit, like signs, wonders, miracles and healings do. The bedrock of scriptural authority rests upon its supreme Author, God. Scripture is used to test signs, wonders, healings and miracles; the miraculous is not a test for the Scriptures.

The miraculous is the greatest living sign and witness

to the gospel. Miracles are part of the convicting tools of the Holy Spirit. Nothing compares to these works as a witnessing instrument for the redemptive work of Christ.

THE GOSPELS SUPPORT THE MIRACULOUS FOR TODAY

Matthew, Mark, Luke and John support the idea that signs and wonders continue today. They imply that all the gifts of the Spirit are continuing still. Paul demands that we follow the example of Christ as portrayed in the Gospels. Since Jesus' ministry used the gifts of the Spirit, we are to do as He did. (See 1 Corinthians 4:16–17; Philippians 3:17; 2 Thessalonians 3:9.) God had specific purposes in mind for these supernatural gifts.

PURPOSES OF THE GIFTS

✝ To convince unbelievers of the truth of God's Word. (See John 14:11.)

✝ To bring glory to God. (See Mark 2:12; Luke 13:17; John 11:4.)

✝ To inspire faith and courage in the very saints of God.

✝ To deliver people from demon possession. (See Matthew 4:24; 8:16, 28, 33; Luke 8:36; Mark 1:32; 5:8; 9:25.)

✝ To perform miracles of nature. (See Mark 4:39; Revelation 6–18.)

✝ To provide for those in want. (See Exodus 17; Mark 6:41–47; 1 Kings 17:15; 18:41; 19:1–7.)

✝ To carry out divine judgments and disciplines. (See Acts 5:5–10; 12:20–23; 1 Corinthians 5:1–5.)

✝ To confirm the preached Word. (See Acts 13:11–12.)

✝ To raise the dead. (See Matthew 10:8; John 11:14–41.)

✝ To display God's power and magnificence. (See Matthew 11:5; John 5:36; 10:25.)

✝ To aid in delivering the afflicted, oppressed and tormented. (See Acts 10:38; Mark 5:5.)

✝ To discover a servant of the devil. (See Acts 13:9–10.)

✝ To aid in stopping the plans of the adversary. (See Acts 16:16.)

✝ To expose error and heresy. (See 1 Timothy 4:1; 2 Peter 2:1.)

✝ To reveal demon miracle-workers. (See 2 Thessalonians 2:9.)

✝ To be blessed. (See Genesis 27:28; Hebrews 11:20.)

✝ For supernatural sustenance in famine or fasting. (See 1 Kings 17:3–4, 23.)

✝ To receive the astounding promises of God and hold on to them. (See Genesis 21:5; Romans 4:20.)

✝ For supernatural victory in the fight. (See Exodus 17:11.)

✝ To assist in domestic and industrial problems. (See 2 Kings 4:1–7.)

✝ Speaking unto men supernaturally. (See 1 Corinthians 14:3.)

✝ For exhortation. (See 1 Corinthians 14:3.)

✝ For comfort. (See 1 Corinthians 14:3, 31.)

✝ So that the saints may learn and know. (See 1 Corinthians 14:31.)

✝ To show God's greatness to an unbeliever. (See 1 Corinthians 14:24–25.)

✝ To make manifest the secrets of the heart. (See 1 Corinthians 14:24–25.)

✝ To teach men. (See 1 Corinthians 14:2–3.)

✝ To make clear. (See 1 Corinthians 14:3–4.)

✝ For foretelling of an event, condition, situation and the like in the future. (See Acts 11:28; Matthew 24–25; 2 Timothy 3:1; Revelation 1–22;

Ezekiel 36:24–35; Daniel 8:9–14, 23–25; 9:24–27; 12:4.)

THE GIFTS BELONG TO THE SPIRIT

The Holy Spirit gives gifts and their manifestations. (See 1 Corinthians 12:7–11.) We cannot operate in them or use them apart from the Holy Spirit. We must therefore submit to the will of the Holy Spirit so that the gifts can be manifested through us. (See 1 Corinthians 14:32.) The Holy Spirit is not a dictator, but uses only willing vessels for His gifts. These gifts are imparted by the Holy Spirit to people as He wills, and He is the only One who will take them away. (See 1 Corinthians 12:7–11; Romans 1:11.)

The believer is the recipient of a gift and is an active partner in the manifestation of the Holy Spirit. Those who experience the gifts of the Spirit are not robbed of their self-consciousness or their self-control, but are in a state of passive receptivity. (See 1 Corinthians 14:32.)

GIFTS NOT LIMITED TO APOSTLES

Paul said that supernatural gifts are necessary for the health of Christ's body. (See 1 Corinthians 12:4–11.) These gifts were not just limited to the twelve apostles. (See Hebrews 11:4–12:3; 1 Corinthians 1:1; 4:16–17; 1 Thessalonians 1:6.) Others who used the Holy Spirit's gifts were those at Pentecost, the Samaritans, Cornelius and the gentiles with him, the disciples at Ephesus, the prophet Agabus, individuals in Acts 13:1, Judas and Silas, the disciples at Tyre, Philip's four unmarried daughters and Ananias. (See Acts 2; 8:18; 9:10–18; 10:45–46; 11:28; 15:32; 19:6; 21:4, 9, 10–11.) Paul, Barnabas, Joseph of Arimathæa, Timothy, Epaphroditus, Mnason of Cyprus, Aquila, Priscilla, James, Andronicus, Junia, disciples of Cæsarea and others were all endowed with the gifts of the Spirit. (See Acts 9:10; 14:4–14; 15:13–19; 16:1; 18:2, 18, 26; 21:16; Galatians 1:19; 1 Corinthians 15:7; 16:19; 1 Thessalonians 2:7; John 19:38; Philippians 2:25; Romans 16:3, 7; 2 Timothy 4:19.)

ATTEMPT TO DELETE GIFTS
FROM THE CHURCH

There has been an attempt by Satan to delete all traces of the supernatural from the Christian's life through the use of tradition. If this is allowed to continue, the church will become weaker and weaker without the power to reveal the enemies of God and the saints.

The Scripture that reads, "Jesus Christ the same yesterday, and today, and forever" signifies that Christ's divine nature is forever the same and, as such, He is a changeless God (Heb. 13:8). The purpose of this verse is not to prove the continuation of the gifts but to prove that Jesus Christ is God. Therefore, the Greek text is dealing with the divine Person who became Man, not His plans or means of operation.

A God who does no works must be considered nonexistent or dead. Christ said that God is not the God of the dead, but of the living. He is the God of the present and not the past. (See Matthew 22:32; 12:37; Luke 20:28.)

UNDERSTANDING MARK 16:17-18

Mark 16:17-18 states that those who are believers will cast out demons, speak with new tongues, have immunity from the bite of snakes and power over them.

This passage must be considered in the light of Greek grammar. Actually, the Greek text strongly states that some saints may not experience any of these things by their own choice. In other words, the saints may or may not enjoy the power and the majesty of the gifts of the Holy Spirit in their lives. It is left up to them, not to God.

SKEPTICS OF CHRIST'S DAY AND THE PRESENT

The skeptics of Christ's day accused Him of casting out demons through Beelzebub. (See Matthew 12:27; Mark 3:22; Luke 11:15-19.) The philosophy of the skeptics of today has not changed. There are those today who deny all divine manifestations. If one denies all divine manifestation, then one must deny salvation and the Scriptures as well. God forbid!

WHY TEST THE SPIRITS

Why would John warn the saints to test every spirit if the supernatural gifts of God would shortly come to an end? (See 1 John 4:1–3) If all of these manifestations were of Satan, John would not have had to warn the saints to judge each spirit. The very notion that John would warn the church not to accept every supernatural manifestation but to try each experience by the Word of God confirms that he recognized no end to these godly and genuine manifestations.

UNDERSTANDING I JOHN 5:5–10

In 1 John 5:5–10, John tells all the saints that the Word of God must agree with the Holy Spirit and the Holy Spirit must agree with the Word of God. This is true with modern manifestations of God's power and miraculous dealings with mankind. When an angel of God comes forth to preach or teach anything by the direct commission of the Holy Spirit, what he does will always completely agree with the Word of God. A demonic spirit can be identified by his use of a teaching that does not agree completely with the Word of God. Parts of a message by a satanic being or even a demon may agree with the Word of God so that the recipient more easily accepts the main parts of the message. The rest, however, will always be filled with lies.

This concept of judging present manifestations of the supernatural by the Word of God was understood and practiced within the early church. They never accepted manifestations of the supernatural without judging them by the Word of God. They saw the Word of God as the test or measuring stick for such manifestations. Condemnation awaited those that placed supernatural manifestations above the Word of God.

One example is Dionysius, bishop of Alexandria, who received a divine word through a vision and decided to accept it because it agreed with Scripture. He writes:

> But I examined the works and traditions of the
> heretics, defiling my mind for a little time with
> their abominable opinions, but receiving this ben-
> efit from them, that I refuted them by myself, and
> detested them all the more. And when a certain
> brother among the presbyters restrained me,
> fearing that I should be carried away with the filth
> of their wickedness (for it would defile my soul)—
> in which also, as I perceived, he spoke the truth—a
> vision sent from God came and strengthened me.
> And the word which came to me commanded me,
> saying distinctly, "Read everything which thou
> canst take in hand, for thou are able to correct and
> prove all; and this has been to thee from the begin-
> ning the cause of thy faith." I received the vision as
> agreeing with the apostolic word [written by the
> Apostles as Scripture]...[8]

Dionysius received this prophetic word more than a
hundred years after the supernatural gifts of the Holy
Spirit are said to have ceased! There was no conflict
between Scripture and the nine supernatural gifts of the
Holy Spirit for the early church. The supernatural gifts
were used to confirm the Word of God, not to supersede it.

The sufficiency of Scripture is confirmed by the miraculous. They are just one proof among many that the Bible
is truly inspired, being the test and judge for all things.
Scripture reveals what is true and what is false, what is of
God and what is not of God. God's Word shows us what we
need to know about God, including all moral commands
and doctrines. It is a clear representation of the will of God
for the Christian and for the rest of the world. It contains
all that is needed to be known about salvation, the future
destiny of the church, the world and the universe. (See 2
Timothy 3:15–16; Acts 17:11; 2 Peter 1:3; Isaiah 8:20.) In
other words, the "sufficiency of Scripture" denotes that
Scripture contains all the words of God that He intended
for His people to possess at each stage of the writing down

of His written Word. It also contains all that we need to know about salvation, trusting God completely, obeying and following Him perfectly and living a holy life before Him.

This does not, however, exclude God from working through His Spirit today to reveal words, comfort, secrets, details, knowledge, wisdom and mysteries to His servants in order to confirm His written Word. (See John 10:27; 14:26; 16:13–14; Romans 8:16; 1 Corinthians 14:29–30; Ephesians 1:17; 1 John 2:27.) This ongoing working of the Holy Spirit includes the continuing revelation of God's purposes for the church and for individuals, and must conform to the written Word. (See Romans 12:6; 1 Corinthians 12:10–28; 14:1–39; Ephesians 4:11; 1 Thessalonians 5:19–21.) The Word of God does not deny or even exhaust the ways that God may speak to His people.

The revelation needed to form and compose the Word of God is not present any longer. But the revelation that takes place through the manifestations of the Holy Spirit, whose sole purpose is to confirm the Word of God, is still alive, well and active. Today's revelation is not that which was present during the composition of the Word of God, nor equal to it. Rather, the revelation now present is a powerful reminder of the revelation of the past, confirming it as being of God. As seen, "revelation" from God has many uses and results. (See Matthew 11:27; Romans 1:18; Philippians 3:15.)

All of this shows that Scripture is indeed sufficient! It must never be considered complete apart from the ministry of Christ and the Holy Spirit. (See John 5:39–40; James 1:5–6; 1 Thessalonians 5:19–22.) The written Word and the Holy Spirit work in agreement always to confirm the validity of each.

UNBELIEVERS

Those who accept that the spiritual gifts of the Holy Spirit are still present and active are often accused of not following the warning given by Christ in Matthew 16:4. The theological problem that the cessationists have is their failure to understand the context of this passage.

According to Matthew 16, it was the Pharisees and Sadducees who came to test Jesus by asking Him to show them a sign from heaven. This is also confirmed in Matthew 12:38–45, Mark 8:11–12, Luke 11:16 and Luke 11:29. This statement or rebuke by Christ is directed toward unbelievers. It was a rebuke and was directed especially against the Jewish leaders who criticized Him. It was not directed to believers who sought a miracle for physical healing, deliverance from demonic oppression or something else from the Lord. I believe it is unbiblical and unethical to apply this passage to believers. There is no New Testament passage that forbids the use of miracles and other manifestations of the Holy Spirit by believers. In fact, the whole New Testament is filled with examples of believers receiving miracles and other benefits from following the Lord. The sign of Jonah, it must be known, is a sign for the unbeliever, not believers. The signs and wonders manifested by the Holy Spirit accompany believers, not unbelievers.

TEST FOR FALSE PROPHETS

Many cessationists warn that those who perform any type of miracle must be false prophets due to the words of Christ. (See Mark 13:22.) But Jesus does not say that all signs and wonders are truly false. Jesus Himself gives a test for false prophets when He says, "You will know them by their fruits" (Matt. 7:16, NKJV). He also states, "My sheep hear my voice, and I know them, and they follow Me" (John 10:27, NKJV).

In reality, Christ does not say in this passage that false prophets will be so deceptive that no Christian would be able to identify them as such. The fact that He would give a warning about false prophets is an indication that genuine signs and wonders would also be present and implies that a saint must learn how to contrast the genuine from the counterfeit.

CONCLUSION

If there are no signs, wonders, healings, miracles or other manifestations of the Spirit within the modern church, then God plays favorites by allowing the early church to experience the outward signs and wonders of His grace and not those saints who came later. Indeed, supernatural visions and revelations are the foundational rocks upon which the church was established and upon which it is sustained. Remove that aspect of the church, and it becomes corrupted and falls. Without these manifestations of God, there is nothing to Christianity. For this reason, the true church, begun in the fire of the Holy Spirit, is sustained with the fire of the Holy Spirit and is the very cradle that holds and nurses the church.

In this chapter, I have attempted to show that there is nothing at all within the Scripture that supports the notion that the gifts and their manifestations have vanished from the earth and the church. Rather, the Scriptures, especially through a close examination of the Greek language and grammar, support and uplift the notion that the gifts and their manifestations must continue in order for the church to be healthy and full of life. Whenever the gifts and their manifestations are denied, the church becomes a lifeless shell of its former glory and beauty. When this happens, the church becomes inferior to what it was because of its denial of the gifts. In order to receive what the early church had, we must be open to receive the gifts and their manifestations. Through prayer we can experience the power released by these same gifts. Only by doing this can the church in its entirety be revived to its former glory and beauty. Oh God, let Your church move in this area and see the glory and beauty which it had in its beginning!

CHAPTER TWO

Historical Evidence for the Gifts

H istory proves that the spiritual gifts have been, and are continuing to be, in operation long after the apostolic age ended. One can easily detect manifestations of these gifts in the fifth through ninth centuries, as well as into the present century. The reason that spiritual gifts almost completely disappeared from the church is due to the presence of formalism, worldliness and lack of prayer that were exhibited at that time in the church. It is not, as some believe, due to the withdrawal of the gifts by the Holy Spirit. The early church, as well as Revivalists like John Wesley, dogmatically taught that the supernatural gifts of the Holy Spirit and their outward manifestations had not yet ended. The Protestant Reformation, in contrast, changed many aspects of church life and practice. The reformers in the beginning, however, never considered the many superfluous practices that had swept the church. They also did not understand that there needed to be a rethinking of Christian doctrine and a return to primitive Christianity as a means of reestablishing the church that God originated. They did not want the Holy Spirit to have His same place in the church as He had in an earlier time. The results of this attitude were more criticism, liberalism, cults of every kind, atheism, secularism, modernism and a host of other ills.

THE REFORMERS

Martin Luther, for example, believed that healing, casting out demons, miracles and other manifestations had ended so that other works, such as teaching and conversion could be done.[1] However, when Luther was confronted with a demon-possessed boy, his opinion about spiritual gifts greatly changed. He saw firsthand how God moved through prayer when the demon within the boy was exorcised.[2] Further, Luther himself, in explaining his *Ninety-Five Theses,* declared that a saint can also still experience visions, trances and other forms of heavenly enlightenment.[3] What a contradiction!

John Calvin was more forceful in his opinion about the supernatural gifts of the Holy Spirit. He concluded that they were destroyed at the close of the apostolic age.[4] Even today, the most forceful opposition against the continuation of the supernatural gifts of the Holy Spirit comes from the encampment of Calvinism. Calvin's disdain for the supernatural seems to continue through the followers of his teaching.

It seems that the reformers, such as Luther and Calvin, did not know their own history. For a hundred years before the Reformation, prophecy was being proclaimed about a great revival that would revitalize the decayed church. John Huss, a predecessor of the Reformation, was burned at the stake for proclaiming the truth of the gospel against the corrupt and perverted church of the times. He prophesied to his enemies that the true church would be revived. He wrote, "After a hundred years has come and gone, they should give account to God and to me."[5] From 1415, when Huss was burned at the stake, and 1416, when a saint known as Jerome also suffered at the stake, to the year 1516 when Martin Luther first began to write, a hundred years was completed. The prophecy of John Huss was thus fulfilled.

Lying in the dungeon of the Friars in Constance shortly before he was to be burned, Huss was given a divinely inspired dream.

> I pray you expound to me the dream which I had this night. I saw that in my church at Bethlehem (whereof I was parson) they desired and labored to abolish all the images of Christ, and did abolish them. I, the next day following, rose up, and saw many other painters, who painted both the same, and many more images, and more fair, which I was

glad to behold. Whereupon the painters, with the
great multitude of people, said, "Now let the
bishops and priests come, and put out these images
if they can." At which thing done, much people
rejoiced in Bethlehem, and I with them. And rising
up, I felt myself to laugh.[6]

He wrote the details of this dream in a letter to John De
Clum, who prayed for divine inspiration to interpret this
dream. God revealed to him that the enemies of John Huss
would destroy the church at Bethlehem, stopping the
preaching of the gospel therein. Greater preachers than
John Huss would preach the gospel of Christ in truth so
strongly that his enemy, the corrupted and perverted
church of Rome, would not be able to stop it.

Huss prophesied accurately many times about the
coming Reformation over one hundred years before its
birth. Countless other men, and even a woman known as
Katharine, prophesied of the coming revival that became
known as the Reformation. Katharine prophesied:

By these tribulations God, after a secret manner
unknown to men, shall purge his holy church; and
after those things, shall follow such a reformation
of the holy church of God, and such renovation of
the holy pastors that only the cogitation and
remembrance thereof makes my spirit to rejoice in
the Lord. And as I have oftentimes told you hereto-
fore, the spouse, which is now all deformed and
ragged, shall be adorned and decked with most rich
and precious collars of gold and brooches.[7]

Jerome of Prague prophesied as he was dying at the
stake, "After an hundred years you shall answer to God
and me."[8]

Theodoric, bishop of Croatia, lived at about the same
time when Huss and Jerome were martyred. At the end of
his prophetical verses, which are extant in print, he
declared the following with great boldness, holy fire and
clearness of thought by the inspiration of the Holy Spirit:

> That the see of Rome, which is so horribly polluted
> with simony and avarice, shall fall, and no more
> oppress men with tyranny, as it hath done, and that
> it shall be subverted by its own subjects; and that
> the church and true piety shall flourish more again,
> than ever it did before.[9]

Dr. Weselus, a Friesian in 1520, prophesied that he should live to see this new school of divinity of Scotus, Aquinas and Bonaventure, to be utterly forsaken and exploded of all true Christians.[10]

The great "A, B, C Prophecy" is found in the margin of a certain old register that is said to be attributed to William Thorpe, an English Reformer who was imprisoned for his views. It is clearly inspired by the One who lives forever and ever.

A wake, ye ghostly persons, awake, awake,
B oth priest, pope, bishop, and cardinal!
C onsider wisely, what ways ye take,
D angerously being like to have a fall.
E verywhere the mischief of you all,
F ar and near, breaketh out very fast;
G od will needs be revenged at the last.
H ow long have ye the world captived,
I n sore bondage of men's traditions?
K ings and emperors ye have deprived,
L ewdly usurping their chief possessions:
M uch misery ye make in all regions.
N ow your frauds be almost at their latter cast,
O f God sore to be revenged at the last.
P oor people to oppress ye have no shame,
Q uaking for fear of your double tyranny.
R ightful justice ye have put out of frame,
S eeking the lust of your god, the belly.
T herefore I dare you boldly certify,
V ery little though you be thereof aghast.
Y et God will be revenged at the last.[11]

By these and similar prophecies, it is evident that the time was not so far off when God would reform and restore His church.

THE REVIVAL OF ALOGIANISM

It is interesting to note that many scholars and laymen who support the idea that the nine supernatural gifts of the Holy Spirit have ceased do not know that they are partly participating in an ancient heresy known as Alogianism. The Alogians, besides denying the deity of Christ, also stated that the supernatural gifts of the Spirit had ceased at the end of the apostolic age. The Alogians were not the only ones who believed that the supernatural gifts of the Holy Spirit had ceased. The Jews also believed that the supernatural gifts ceased at the close of the Old Testament canon, in the fifth century B.C. It is for this reason that the Jews accused Christ of accomplishing all the signs and wonders through Beelzebub. (See Matthew 12:27; Mark 3:22; Luke 11:15–19.) Yet, Christ proved them wrong!

MARCION AND TERTULLIAN

The heretic, Marcion, also proclaimed that all supernatural gifts had ceased. He was head of a form of Gnosticism known as Asiatic Gnosticism during the third century. Tertullian, an ancient theologian and defender of Christianity, refuted this saying.

> Now all these signs of spiritual gifts are forth-coming from my side of the argument without any difficulty, and they agree, too, with the rules, and the dispensations, and the instructions of the Creator.[12]

To Tertullian, dispensationalism in its early form did not hinder or destroy the idea that the supernatural gifts of the Holy Spirit are still in operation. This pure dispensationalism, as taught by the early church, dictated that the gifts of the Holy Spirit could not cease until perfection had come. Even then, there was a possibility that some gifts might continue indefinitely.

Tertullian, attacking Marcion again about denying the continuation of the gifts and especially those gifts of the prophetic nature, states:

> Consequently, it will be clearly seen of what the apostles spoke, even of those things which were to happen in the church of his God; and as long as He endures, so long also does His Spirit work, and so long are His promises repeated.[13]

What force there is in Tertullian's argument! For Tertullian, those who refute the continuation of the prophetic gifts along with the others, deny that God still endures and His Spirit continues to work. Tertullian accused them of blasphemy and heresy.

In dealing with the authority and power of saints over demons, he writes:

> All the authority and power we have over them is from our naming the name of Christ, and recalling to their memory the woes with which God threatens them at the hands of Christ as Judge, and which they expect one day to overtake them. Fearing Christ in God, and God in Christ, they become subject to the servants of God and Christ. *So by our touch and by our breath*, overwhelmed by the thought and realization of those judgment fires, they leave at our command the bodies they have entered, unwilling, and distressed, and before your very eyes put to an open shame. You believe them when they lie; give credit to them, then, when they speak the truth about themselves. No one plays the liar to bring disgrace upon his own head, but for the sake of honour rather. You give a readier confidence to people making confessions against themselves, than denials in their own behalf.[14]

In another writing, Tertullian again states that multitudes of demoniacs were delivered from their demons by

Christians possessed with the power of God and using the nine supernatural gifts of the Holy Spirit. He speaks further of Christians only, not pagans, having this power to expel demons.[15] He acknowledges the continuation of the supernatural gifts in the third century and mentions that he knows of a sister in Christ who was a prophetess that God favored with gifts of revelation, visions, seeing angels, seeing the Lord, seeing and hearing mysterious communications and understanding men's hearts.[16] He definitely states that the *charismata*, which are the gifts of the Spirit, are for all children of God, not just the apostles and that even Christ spoke in unknown tongues. [17]

Tertullian also mentions new prophecies that God gave.[18] In the document known as "The Constitutions of the Holy Apostles" that was completely compiled before 325 A.D., there is a clear recognition of the "continuation of all the supernatural gifts of the Holy Spirit." In addition, it states that the gifts themselves were not only given to the apostles, but also to others who believed after them. The point here is that the gifts of the Holy Spirit are not just for the apostles, but for the saints.[19]

BLOWING OR BREATHING UPON PEOPLE

The tradition of blowing or breathing upon people seems to have been founded by Jesus Himself according to John 20:22. This breath represents power or blessing being bestowed. According to Augustine, the apostles received the Holy Spirit when Jesus blew upon them.[20] The Gospel of Thomas speaks of Jesus blowing upon Thomas to be healed of a snakebite.[21] The early church interpreted John 3:8 and John 20:22 as firm proof that the blowing or breathing upon people is scriptural. On the last page of this work, Tertullian mentioned this same tradition of breathing upon people. It reveals in his statement the power of God so released that demons fled.

APOSTOLIC FATHER IGNATIUS

Ignatius, a pupil of the apostles in the first century, and

recognized as a prophet of God, wrote to the Philippians, "And there is also one Paraclete. For 'there is also,' saith the scripture, 'one Spirit,' since 'we have been called in one hope of our calling.' And again, 'we have drunk of one Spirit,' with which follows. And it is manifest that all these gifts possessed by believers 'worketh one and the selfsame Spirit.'"[22] This is an independent source that shows that the supernatural gifts were in operation within the apostolic age.

Ignatius, in his epistle to the Philadelphians, prophesies to them and says, "Do nothing without the bishop; keep your bodies as the temples of God; love unity; avoid divisions; be followers of Jesus Christ, even as He is of His Father."[23]

JUSTIN MARTYR

Justin Martyr, who was a second-century theologian and defender of Christianity against Judaism, states very clearly that the supernatural gifts were alive and well after the deaths of the twelve apostles.

> For the prophetical gifts remain with us, even to the present time. And hence you ought to understand that the gifts formerly among your nation have been transferred to us...Now it is possible to see amongst us women and men who possesses gifts of the Spirit of God...For we call him [Christ] helper and redeemer, the power of whose name even the demons do fear; and at this day, when they are exorcized in the name of Jesus Christ...they are overcome...For numberless demoniacs throughout the whole world, and in your city, many of our Christian men exorcizing them in the name of Jesus Christ.[24]

IRENÆUS

Irenæus, also a pupil of a student of the apostle John, wrote in the second century:

> And so far are they from being able to raise the dead, as the Lord raised them, and the apostles did

by means of prayer, and as has been frequently
done in the brotherhood on account of some neces-
sity—the entire church in that particular locality
entreated [the boon] with much fasting and prayer,
the spirit of the dead man has returned...For some
do certainly and truly drive out devils, so that those
who have thus been cleansed from evil spirits frequently both believe in Christ, and join themselves
to the church. Others have foreknowledge of things
to come: They see visions, and utter prophetic
expressions. Others still, heal the sick by laying
their hands upon them, and they are made whole.
Yet, moreover, as I have said, the dead even have
been raised up, and remained among us for many
years...that the gift of prophecy is not conferred on
men by Marcus, the magician, but that only those to
whom God sends His grace from above possess the
divinely-bestowed power of prophesying; and then
they speak where and when God pleases.[25]

Again, Irenæus sets forth that supernatural gifts are still
in existence.

For this reason does the apostle declare, "We
speak wisdom among them that are perfect,"
terming those persons "perfect" who have
received the Spirit of God, and who through the
Spirit of God do speak in all languages, as he used
Himself also to speak. In like manner we do also
hear many brethren in the church, who possess
prophetic gifts, and who through the Spirit speak
all kinds of languages, and bring to light for the
general benefit the hidden things of men, and
declare the mysteries of God, whom also the
apostle terms "spiritual," they being spiritual
because they partake of the Spirit, and not because
their flesh has been stripped off and taken away,
and because they have become purely spiritual.[26]

He also states that God bestows many gifts on those
who please Him.[27]

RECEPTION OF THE HOLY SPIRIT AND CYPRIAN

It is remarkable that the early church felt very strongly that the baptism of the Holy Spirit, also known as the reception of the Spirit, was not the baptism into Christ, but something following it. The baptism into Christ denotes that a person has been united in fellowship with Christ by means of repentance and the new birth. (See Romans 6:3–7; 1 Corinthians 12:13; Galatians 3:27; Colossians 2:12.) The baptism of the Holy Spirit was seen as separate from salvation. The great theologian Cyprian writes:

> For if the apostle does not speak falsely when he says, "As many of you as are baptized into Christ, have put on Christ," certainly he who has been baptized among them into Christ, has put on Christ. But if he has put on Christ, he might also receive the Holy Ghost, who was sent by Christ, and hands are vainly laid upon him who comes to us for the reception of the Spirit; unless, perhaps, he has not put on the spirit from Christ, so that Christ indeed may be with heretics, but the Holy Spirit not be with them.[28]

GIFTS, DEMONS AND GOD'S VOICE

Cyprian, who was a cultist before his conversion, mentions in the third century that demons were constantly being cast off by Christians and as such were under the power of Christians.[29] He also writes about the supernatural gifts and their manifestations.

> For this reason the divine rebuke does not cease to chastise us night nor day. For besides the visions of the night, by day also, the innocent age of boys is among us filled with the Holy Spirit, seeing in an ecstasy with their eyes, and hearing and speaking those things whereby the Lord condescends to warn and instruct us. And you shall hear all things which the Lord, who bade me withdraw, shall bring me back again to you.[30]

He debunks the idea that God's voice is not heard any longer in writing, "Now speak with God, now let God speak with you, He himself instruct you in his precepts, let him direct you."[31]

In 160 A.D., Hermas, an apostolic leader of the church, wrote that there were still present among the churches prophets and apostles whose lives were to be tested to see if they were of God.[32] This document, known as the *Didache*, also recognizes apostles other than the twelve and prophets as a very important part of the church. In addition, it recognizes the continuation of the divine gifts and the offices of apostles and prophets.[33]

Melito, the bishop of Sardis in the late second century, prophesied in the midst of a famous sermon.

> Who will contend against me; Let him stand before me. It is I who delivered the condemned. It is I who gave life to the dead. It is I who raised up the buried. Who will argue with me? It is I, says Christ, who destroyed death. It is I who triumphed over the enemy, and trod down Hades, and bound the strong man, and have snatched mankind up to the heights of heaven. It is I, says Christ. So then come here all you families of men, weighed down by your sins, and receive pardon for your misdeeds. For I am your pardon. I am the Passover which brings salvation. I am the lamb slain for you. I am your lustral bath. I am your life. I am your resurrection. I am your light. I am your salvation. I am your king. It is I who bring you up to the heights of heaven. It is I who give your resurrection there. I will show you the eternal Father. I will raise you up with my own right hand.[34]

MONTANUS AND MONTANISM

The Christian group called the Montanists was founded by Montanus in the second century in the province of Phrygias in Asia Minor. This group manifested all the spiritual gifts of the Holy Spirit. However, during their early existence, counterfeit gifts began to surface that started to destroy this group of faithful Christians. These counterfeit gifts and the fact that fewer people were becoming Montanists, led to its extinction in the ninth century.

Also, aiding in the eradication of the Montanists was the fact that a heretic named Praxeas brought forth accusations against them and against their use of the spiritual gifts and the gifts themselves. He tried to say that both the genuine and counterfeit gifts were of the same nature and of the same source. Because of Praxeas, the church in general rejected the Montanists and the genuine gifts that flowed within that group. Tertullian was part of this group and defended it with boldness and righteous anger. He declared:

> For after the Bishop of Rome had acknowledged the prophetic [and spiritual] gifts of Montanus, Prisca, and Maximilla, and, in consequence of the acknowledgment, had bestowed his peace on the churches of Asia and Phrygia, he [Praxeas], by importunately urging false accusations against the prophets themselves and their churches, and insisting on the authority of the bishop's predecessors in the see, compelled him to recall the pacific letter which he had issued, as well as to desist from his purpose of acknowledging the said gifts. By this Praxeas did a twofold service, for the devil at Rome: he drove away prophecy [probably other gifts as well] and brought in heresy; he put to flight the Paraclete [Holy Spirit], and he crucified the Father.[35]

While there were counterfeit gifts within Montanism, one cannot dismiss the genuine gifts that flowed through this group until the ninth century. Genuine and godly Montanism stressed a strong faith in the Holy Spirit. It emphasized the Holy Spirit manifesting Himself supernaturally through His gifts with a strong morality and discipline.

ORIGEN AND HIPPOLYTUS

Origen, writing against Celsus in the third century, states that the nine supernatural gifts were still preserved in the

church even during his day. He reminds Celsus, a skeptic
of Christianity, of the marvelous power of these gifts by the
cures that many Christians were performing and
receiving. He tells him that many persons had been freed
from grievous calamities, madness, demon possession and
countless other ills. Origen himself says that he is an eyewitness of these events.[36]

In the canons of Hippolytus, who was an ecclesiastical
writer in the third century, the gifts of healing are mentioned as still being in existence.[37]

THE GIFTS PROVE CHRISTIAN FAITH

Arnobius was a Christian defender of the faith who
wrote in opposition to those who were heathen. He found
support for Christianity by the continued use of the gifts
within the Christian community. In his work, he states:

> Who [Christ] appears even now to righteous men of
> unpolluted mind who love him, not in airy dreams,
> but in a form of pure simplicity; whose name, when
> heard puts to flight evil spirits, imposes silence on
> soothsayers, prevents men from consulting the
> augurs [false prophets], causes the efforts of arro-
> gant magicians to be frustrated, not by the dread of
> his name, as you allege, but by the free exercise of
> a greater power.[38]

Saint Isidore declared that all the gifts of the Holy Spirit
would continue until the coming of the Antichrist. He
wrote, "Before Antichrist does appear, all virtues and signs
shall cease from the church."[39] Saint Gregory stated the
same thing. He wrote, "For by a terrible ordering of God's
secret dispensation shall all signs of virtue or power be
withdrawn from the holy church, before that Leviathan
appear in that damnable man."[40]

GODLY MEN IN THE FOURTH AND FIFTH CENTURIES

In particular, notice that godly men in the fourth and fifth centuries, such as Jerome, Gregory of Nyssa, Athanasius, Chrysostom, Ambrose and Augustine, all admit that miracles continued in their days.

A work completed in the fourth century entitled *Two Epistles Concerning Virginity*, gives advice about the use of gifts within the church.

> But if thou hast received "the word of knowledge, or the word of instruction, or of prophecy," blessed be God, "who helps every man without grudging—that God who gives to every man and does not unbraid him." With the gift, therefore, which thou hast received from our Lord, serve thy spiritual brethren, the prophets who know that the words which thou speakest are those of our Lord; and declare the gift which thou hast received in the church for the edification of the brethren in Christ (for good and excellent are those things which help the men of God), if so be that they are truly with thee.[41]

This work confirms that there were prophets in the church even during the fourth century and that the nine supernatural gifts of the Holy Spirit were also still in use.

In the fourth century, it was reported that Pachomius, the founder of Cenobitic Christian Monasticism, spoke in tongues that were unknown by him.[42]

Cyril, who was the bishop of Jerusalem in the fourth century, recognized that exorcisms were still in operation within the church. He also believed that the gift of prophecy was still in operation. He expressed hope that his reader would be worthy to receive the gift of prophecy.[43]

Ambrose, also a bishop of Milan in the fourth century, writes:

> That many are cleansed from evil spirits, that very many also, having touched with their hands the

> robe of the saints, are freed from those ailments,
> which oppressed them; you see that the miracles of
> old time are renewed, when through the coming of
> the Lord Jesus grace was more largely shed forth
> upon the earth, and that many bodies are healed as
> it were by the shadow of the holy bodies. How many
> napkins are passed about![44]

In 337 A.D. the city of Nisibis was sieged. Ephraem, a biblical and ecclesiastical writer, asked God to bring judgment upon the Persians by a host of gnats and mosquitoes. His prayer was instantly answered by a cloud of these insects, tiny yet unavoidable assailants, descending on the enemy. Maddened by this plague, the horses flung their riders, the elephants broke free and trampled down the men, and the camp was thrown into confusion. A storm of wind, rain and thunder enhanced the panic, and the Persian general was forced to end the siege and retreat. Ephraem is recorded to have had several visions and to have brought about several other miracles through the power of God.

Hilary, Bishop of Poitiers, confessed that the working of signs and wonders still continued in the fourth century.[45] Bishop Basil at this same time said that Gregory, the bishop of Neocæsarea, was great in working signs and wonders. He was known also as "Gregory Thaumaturgus," or "Gregory the Wonder-Worker." Notice what Basil says about Gregory: "So great was the Spirit upon him that demons trembled at his presence. He commanded rivers to change their course and caused a lake to dry up. He had such a strong gift of prophecy that he was compared to the Twelve Apostles and Old Testament Prophets. He was known as a second Moses."[46] In the ecclesiastical history of Socrates, it is recounted that Gregory cast out demons just by writing letters to those who were possessed.[47]

In church history, Eusebius also retells many signs and wonders that were worked by God long after the end of the apostolic age. Attalus was visited by God in a vision. Many miracles were worked throughout the whole church. God sent rain from heaven for Marcus Aurelius Cæsar in answer to the prayers of Christians. The whole church in one voice confirmed that miracles were still continuing. Christians had been prewarned to leave Jerusalem before Titus put it under siege. Dionysius received a divine word through a vision and decided to accept it because it agreed with Scripture. The miracles of Narcissus were recorded as well.[48]

In Eusebius' history of Constantine, he recounts that the cross appeared to Constantine, and upon it was written "Conquer by This." Constantine also had a vision of Christ.[49] He recounted countless martyrs that manifested, by the power of the Holy Spirit, a supernatural laughter that was many times uncontrollable. This genuine laughter seems to also be continuing.[50]

Athanasius, who was the bishop of Alexandria, wrote in the fourth century about several miracles. He states very definitely that he himself knew bishops who worked wonders:[51]

> And it is not fitting to boast at the casting forth of the demons, nor to be uplifted by the healing of diseases; nor is it fitting that he who casts out devils should alone be highly esteemed, while he who casts them not out should be considered nought. But let each man learn the discipline of each one and either imitate, rival, or correct it. For the working of signs is not ours but the Saviour's work. But we ought always to pray, as I said above, that we may receive the gift of discerning spirits.[52]

It was also reported by Athanasius that the hermit, Saint Antony, had control over animals, healed the sick, rebuked and expelled many demons from those who were possessed and had several visions while under the power of God.[53]

Augustine, the bishop of Hippo in the fifth century, at first denied that the supernatural gifts were still in operation. He then later reversed this opinion. He changed his mind because he had become an eyewitness to the supernatural gifts in operation. One of his observations was of a man known as "John the Monk." Augustine says that this man was gifted with the gift of prophecy, as well as other gifts.[54]

In his work entitled *The City of God*, Augustine speaks strongly about miracles and their continuation and concludes that they had not yet ceased.[55] This is the same man who at one time believed that the gifts and all their manifestations had ended.[56] He also states in this same work that he witnessed more than seventy recorded and verified instances of miracles in less than two years in his city of Hippo alone.

After his change of views, he wrote the following in reference to the gift of tongues and his new endowment of power from the Holy Spirit:

> We still do what the apostles did when they laid hands on the Samaritans, and called down the Holy Spirit on them by the laying on of hands. It is expected that converts should speak with new tongues.[57]

This was such a strong influence upon his life and his views that it changed him forever. The only well-known bishop at the time who rejected the idea that the supernatural gifts of the Holy Spirit and their manifestations were in operation was Chrysostom, the bishop of Constantinople.[58]

During the fifth century, John Cassian, a monk who dealt with divine gifts, added to our understanding. He elucidates in the *Discourse of Abbot Nesteros* on the threefold system of gifts. He believed that because the gifts are still present within the saints, the world should admire them. He related a case where Abbot Macarius raised a dead man, and a lame man was cured. Cassian also felt that miracles should not be the test by which each person's merits are judged. He believed that the excellence of the gifts consists not so much in miracles, but humility. He exhorted Christians to cast out their own faults rather than demons. He said that to live righteously is more important than working miracles.[59] He also testified that John the Monk had the gift of prophecy.[60]

Sulpit(c)ius Severus, an apostle of Austria in the fifth century, wrote a biography of Saint Martin of Tours. The life of this man is so very remarkable. Notice the supernatural experiences of Martin:

✞ Christ Himself appeared to Martin in a vision.

✞ Satan himself appeared to him.

✞ Through the power of God, he raised up someone who had been strangled to death.

✞ Pagans, intending to kill Martin, bound him up under a pine tree and cut down the tree so that it would fall upon him, but the power of God intervened. Martin's hand was set free and raised above his bindings. At that instant the falling tree spun to the opposite direction and almost crashed upon the pagans.

✞ Martin had control over fire and kept it from destroying a house.

✞ One pagan, while trying to kill Martin, was struck to the ground by the power of God and became overwhelmed by the fear of God. He retreated and stopped the attack against Martin.

✞ Another pagan sought to kill Martin with a knife, but at the moment of striking Martin, the weapon was struck out of his hands by the power of God. The weapon disappeared from sight and was never seen again.

✞ Many miracles occurred through Martin's ministry, such as resurrection, healings of paralysis and infirmity, and countless others.

✞ Martin cast out many demons.

✞ He performed many other types of miracles.

✞ He saw many angels and demons.[61]

Severus in *Dialogues* writes:

I shudder to state what I have lately heard, that a miserable man (I know him not) has said that you have told many lies in that book of yours (about Martin). This is not the voice of a man, but the devil;

and it is not Martin who is, in this way, injured, but faith is taken from the Gospels themselves. For, since the Lord himself testified of works of the kind which Martin accomplished, that they were to be performed by all the faithful, he who does not believe that Martin accomplished such deeds, simply does not believe that Christ uttered such words.[62]

In the ecclesiastical history of the church, historian Sozomen in the fifth century records the prophecy given by John the Monk. In this fulfilled prophecy, he states that the war facing the Emperor of Rome would terminate in his favor and that the tyrant Eugenius would be slain. After the victory the emperor himself would die in Italy.[63]

Furthermore, Sozomen records the signs and wonders wrought by many godly men through the power of God during the fourth and fifth centuries. For example, Amon was able to discern the future and most hidden things as clearly as the ancient prophets were and was endowed with the gifts of healing. The saints Copres, Helles and Eulogius all wrought many kinds of miracles. Copres, for example, was endowed with the gift of prophecy. Eulogius was said to know men's minds and what they thought.[64]

Socrates, another fifth-century church historian, records an account of a Christian who accomplished so many cures and cast out so many demons that it would require a whole book to recount all that was done.[65] He also reports the banishment of the superiors of several monks who were endowed with supernatural power.[66] According to Socrates, one Frumentius, the apostle of the Abyssinians in India, performed various miracles and healing.[67]

GREAT PROPHETIC MOVEMENTS

The greatest prophetic movement during that time was the Ascetic movement. It swept through the church in Egypt and Asia Minor and continued until the ninth century. There were numerous accounts of prophecies, exorcisms and miracles.

The second great prophetic movement was in the Western Church in the twelfth and thirteenth centuries. This consisted of the Cistercian movement, which arose in France during the twelfth century, and the Franciscan and Dominican movements that arose in Italy in the thirteenth century.

Between 1000 and 1453 A.D. the Hesychasm movement in the Eastern Church was endowed with the gift of prophecy manifested through many persons.

MANIFESTATIONS OF GIFTS IN MODERN REVIVALS

Tongues appeared in many of the great revivals throughout the centuries. The Waldensians (eleventh and twelfth centuries), Jansenists (seventeenth century), Quakers (seventeenth century), Shakers (eighteenth century), and Methodists (eighteenth century) all spoke in unknown tongues and had other manifestations of supposedly dead gifts.

Between 1825 and 1830, a great renewal of the gifts and their manifestations took place in Scotland. Visions, shaking, fainting, tongues, healings and other such manifestations all took place. In 1831, Edward Irving in Scotland experienced the gifts and their manifestations during another revival in Scotland.

In the ministry of Dwight L. Moody in 1873, spiritual gifts also made an appearance. This included not only the gift of tongues, but also prophecy so accurate that no one could discount them as being genuine.[68]

Further, in the 1800s, Johaun Blunhardt, John Morgan, William Arthur, Carles Cullis, Otto Stockmayer, Asa Mahan and other notable figures all experienced the refreshing of the Holy Spirit through His gifts and their manifestations.

H. A. Baker, a missionary to China in the early dawning of the twentieth century, witnessed one of the greatest outpourings of the Spirit. Visions, revelations, dreams, tongues, healings and other such gifts were strongly manifested through children and young people.[69]

In the revival at Cane Ridge, Kentucky, in 1801, part of the Second Great Awakening, cries and shouts of repentance were heard for miles. The crying of babies, the shrieking of children and the neighing of horses were heard as well because of God's power. Along with this came other supernatural experiences. Some people fell down while others only experienced weakened knees or a light head. Some fell but remained conscious or talkative. A few fell into a deep coma, displaying the symptoms of a grand mal seizure. It was said that the ground was strewn with bodies like a battlefield. Others reported that sinners ran to the altar while shrieking, groaning and crying for salvation. Moans, clapping, hugging and laughing all were heard. Some were attended to where they fell while others were carried to a convenient place where people would gather around them to pray and sing hymns. Some uncontrollably jerked their heads. A seven-year-old girl who could not speak well spoke eloquent words, which could not have come from her without the Spirit giving utterance.[70] This revival increased from twenty thousand to approximately forty thousand people within a few months.

John Wesley believed in the supernatural gifts and their manifestations. He spoke of an incident that occurred in France during his lifetime where tongues fell upon the Protestant inhabitants of several valleys.[71] Unequivocally, Wesley experienced many manifestations of the Holy Spirit throughout his ministry. His journals are filled with experiences from the Holy Spirit. Healings, falling out by the Spirit, prophecy, speaking in unknown tongues, casting out demons, trembling exceedingly by the power of God, strong convulsions and crying are all mentioned by him as occurring in his services.[72] He also recalls hearing heavenly sounds that no human could have made.[73]

Skeptics of the continuance of the spiritual gifts will deny Wesley's own words and point to a place in Wesley's journals where he attacks uncontrolled laughter as proof that he was against all supernatural manifestations.[74] Wesley, however, only opposed counterfeit manifestations that were from Satan. He did oppose unholy laughter, whether natural or spiritual. There is no proof that he rejected holy laughter that was initiated by the Holy Spirit. Where there are genuine manifestations, counterfeits will follow.

Wesley, in dealing with a cessationist known as Reverend Middleton, said this after the minister declared that the gifts had been withdrawn:

> O Sir, mention this no more. I entreat you, never name their silence again. They speak loud enough to shame you as long as you live.[75]

Wesley elaborates further about another incident on June 15, 1739.

> While I was earnestly inviting all sinners to "enter into the holiest" by this "new and living way," many of those that heard began to call upon God with strong cries and tears. Some sunk down, and there remained no strength in them; others exceedingly trembled and quaked; some were torn with a kind of convulsive motion in every part of their bodies, and that so violently, that often four or five persons could not hold one of them. I have seen many hysterical and many epileptic fits; but none of them were like these in many respects. I immediately prayed that God would not suffer those who were weak to be offended. But one woman was offended greatly; being sure they might help it if they would—no one should persuade her to the contrary; and was got three or four yards, when she also dropped down, in as violent an agony as the rest.[76]

On June 22, 1739, Wesley tells of a time when the outward signs of the Holy Spirit were evident to all that desired to see.

> While I was yet speaking, one before me dropped down as dead, and presently a second and third. Five others sunk down in half-an-hour, most of whom were in violent agonies. The pains as of hell came about them; the snares of death overtook them.[77]

Wesley talked to a Mr. Whitefield on July 7, 1739, who opposed these same outward signs.

> I had an opportunity to talk with Mr. Whitefield of those outward signs which had so often accompanied the inward work of God. I found his objections were chiefly ground on gross misrepresentations of matter of fact. But the next day he had an opportunity of informing himself better: for no sooner had he begun (in the application of his sermon) to invite all sinners to believe in Christ, than four persons sunk down close to him, almost in the same moment. One of them lay without either sense or motion. A second trembled exceedingly. The third had strong convulsions all over his body, but made no noise, unless by groans. The fourth equally conversed called upon God, with strong cries and tears. From this time, I trust, we shall all suffer God to carry on His own work in the way that pleaseth Him.[78]

The Great Awakening, headed by Jonathan Edwards in the eighteenth century, gave the prophetic gifts a voice. During this time there were many other manifestations of the Holy Spirit. Some voiced such concern about these supernatural gifts and their manifestations that they accused the entire Great Awakening movement of being in league with Satan. Jonathan Edwards refuted those accusations and preached on the genuine and counterfeit signs, affirming that what occurred in the Great Awakening was of God. Indeed, he concluded that God could still perform miracles, speak to His people, show dreams and visions, and work all sorts of other manifestations.

In his writings Edwards describes many people in his day who experienced the extraordinary work of the Holy Spirit. He describes one person who continued for five or six hours in a vision of Christ. When the vision ended, it seemed as though only a minute had passed. Extraordinary views of divine things, prophecy, tongues and the like manifested themselves frequently in this revival. For a time some could neither stand nor speak. Others clinched their hands while their flesh became cold even though their senses remained. Many uncontrollably shook and fell to the ground. An extraordinary sense of the awful majesty, greatness and holiness of God overwhelmed the soul and body of all that witnessed these manifestations of the Spirit, and a sense of repentance filled the whole revival.[79]

Edwards expresses much about the continuation of the supernatural gifts of the Holy Spirit and their manifestations, "The whole tenor of the Gospel proves it; all the notion of religion that the scripture gives us confirms it."[80] Indeed, he confesses that if the continuation of the supernatural gifts of the Holy Spirit were not so, then one must reject the whole Bible.[81]

In his work entitled *Marks of a Work of the True Spirit*, Edwards writes about the outward signs of the Holy Spirit in the Great Awakening:

> He has brought to pass new things, strange works; and has wrought in such a manner as to surprise both men and angels. And as God has done thus in times past, so we have no reason to think but that he will do so still.[82]

In this marvelous statement Edwards acknowledges that it is easy for a saint of God to recognize that the same manifestations of God's grace will still be applicable today. By this statement, he shows that the same gifts and experiences that were found in the early church will be found in the modern church as well. He also defends being slain in the Spirit and other manifestations of God's grace.[83]

Even after seeing all the manifestations of God's grace and the continuation of the spiritual gifts, Edwards reversed his opinions. The outpouring of the Holy Spirit contradicted his Calvinistic training and theology. At the beginning of *Marks of a Work of the True Spirit*, Edwards accepted the outward signs of the Holy Spirit, but later denied them all.[84] Once again we see how Calvin's disdain for the supernatural influenced Edwards then and continues today.

This change of opinion by Edwards is to his shame and disgrace! By making this choice, he places dogma above the Word of God. Tradition becomes the stumbling block to his realization that the Holy Spirit continues to work in the supernatural.

Because God the Father and the Word of God still endure, God the Holy Spirit is still working in the world today. Christianity continues to be vibrant and alive, with supernatural manifestations of the Spirit flowing out into the world.

CHAPTER THREE

The Overshadowing of the Spirit

A s we saw in the previous chapter, John Wesley experienced many strange and varied works of God relating to spiritual gifts. Long before Wesley, Saint Augustine dealt with these same manifestations of the Spirit in his midst and wrote:

> Some things are done in one way, others in another, and so that man cannot at all comprehend them— nevertheless, these miracles attest this faith which preaches the resurrection of the flesh to eternal life.[1]

Augustine personally saw what God brought about several years after the gifts of the Holy Spirit and their manifestations supposedly had ceased. Yet, he beheld the glory of God and saw such a variety of miracles that he could not doubt what God had done. God did things in a manner that he had never witnessed before. Augustine never doubted the means and the ways in which God works. His philosophy became, "Whatever God wants and wants to do so be it." This should be upon the breath of every saint.

Wesley experienced many manifestations of the Holy Spirit throughout his ministry including some that were strange and bizarre. He witnessed healings, people falling out by the Spirit, prophecies, speaking in unknown tongues, the casting out of demons, trembling by the power of God, shaking from strong convulsions, crying, tears and heavenly sounds. He saw sinners sink down to the ground because they had no strength. Others trembled and quaked. Some were torn with a kind of convulsive motion in every part of their bodies so that even four or five people could not hold them down.

Jonathan Edwards in *Marks of a Work of the True Spirit,*

again writes about the manifestations of the Spirit during the Great Awakening.

> He has brought to pass new things, strange works; and has wrought in such a manner as to surmise both men and angels. And as God has done thus in times past, so we have no reason to think but that he will do so still. The prophecies of Scripture give us reason to think that God has things to accomplish, which have never yet been seen. No deviation from what has hitherto been usual, let it be never so great, is an argument that a work is not from the Spirit of God, if it be no deviation from his prescribed rule. The Holy Spirit is sovereign in his operation; and we know that he uses a great variety; and we cannot tell how great a variety he may use, within the compass of the rules he himself has fixed. We ought not to limit God where he has not limited himself.[2]

Edwards is relating that he himself saw firsthand many manifestations that were outside of what the established church considered the norm. Because of the powerful outpourings of the Holy Spirit, many denounced this movement as coming from Satan. Edwards refuted this and developed criteria to differentiate a true manifestation of God from a counterfeit. He formulated the following criteria:

1. The activity must raise the very esteem of Jesus Christ who was born of the Virgin and was crucified. (See 1 John 4:1–3; 4:15; Matthew 10:32; Romans 15:9; Philippians 2:11; 1 Corinthians 12:3.)

2. The manifestation is used to shine a light upon the gospel of Christ.

3. When such action seems to confirm and establish in the minds of people more than anything else the truth of what the gospel declares to all of Christ being the Son of God and the Savior of men.

4. When a spirit operates against the interests of Satan's kingdom. (See 1 John 4:4–5; 3:8.)

5. When a spirit operates in such a manner as to cause a hunger for the Holy Scriptures, and establishes those who experience this in truth and divinity. (See 1 John 4:6; Ephesians 2:20.)

6. When a spirit operates in such a manner as to lead people into the full truth of the fundamentals. (See 1 John 4:1–6.)

7. When a spirit operates in such a manner as to promote a spirit of love to God and man. (See 1 John 4:6–7.)

8. When a spirit operates in such a manner as to promote agreement with the Holy Scriptures. (See 1 John 5:5–10.)

9. When a spirit operates in such a manner as to promote the holiness, greatness and majesty of God. (See 1 John 5:5–10; 4:1–7; Ephesians 4:24; Luke 1:75; Romans 6:19, 22; Hebrews 12:14; 2 Corinthians 7:1; 1 Thessalonians 4:7; 1 Timothy 2:15; Titus 2:5; 1 Peter 14:16; Hebrews 12:10; Galatians 5:14; 6:2; 1 Corinthians 7:19; Romans 8:4; 12:2; 13:8–10; Philippians 1:11; 1 Thessalonians 3:13; 4:3–7; 5:23; 1 Corinthians 1:8; 7:34; 2 Corinthians 7:1.)

10. When a spirit causes unusual and extraordinary events and effects upon the lives, minds and bodies of persons that emphasize the holiness of God, His greatness and His majesty. (See 1 John 5:5–10; 4:1–7; Ephesians 4:24; Luke 1:75; Romans 6:19, 22; Hebrews 12:14; 2 Corinthians 7:1; 1 Thessalonians 3:13; 4:7; 1 Timothy 2:15; Titus 2:5; 1 Peter 14:16; Hebrews 12:10; Galatians 5:14; 6:2; 1 Corinthians 7:19; Romans 8:4; 12:2; 13:8–10; 1 Thessalonians 3:13; 4:3–7; 5:23; 1 Corinthians 1:8; 7:34.)

In manifestations such as these, people will have an extraordinary conviction of their sin nature, an uncommon sense of the Christian life, and extraordinary views of the certainty and glory of divine things. They will be equally moved by feelings of fear and sorrow, desire, love or joy, and can change very suddenly. All of this is in agreement with the Scripture. It also includes tears, trembling, groans, loud outcries, agonies of body, the failing of bodily strength and what has been known as being "slain in the Spirit." All of this coming from God will always be in the realm of God's holiness, His greatness and His majesty.[3]

John, in speaking of the ministry of Jesus, wrote, "And there are also many other things which Jesus did, the which, if they should be written every one, I suppose that even the world itself could not contain the books that should be written" (John 21:25). He makes the point that many manifestations of the Spirit that were done through Christ were never written down. Some of the manifestations of the Spirit that are currently taking place may have also taken place in Christ's ministry, but were not written down in the biblical account.

God says, "Behold, the former things are come to pass, and new things do I declare: before they spring forth I tell you of them" (Isa. 42:9). This verse explicitly deals with the Servant-Messiah. God foretells that along with the Messiah's coming, new things will also be seen that were not seen before. What could be clearer than this? The implication is that God will do different things, never seen before within His church.

In Isaiah 48:6, God says, "Thou hast heard, see all this; and will not ye declare *it*? I have shown thee new things from this time, even hidden things, and thou didst not know them." God is speaking to Israel, telling them that He has revealed new things to them. Yet, they did not heed His words or accept them. It is clear that God manifested new things to His people that they had not seen or witnessed before.

Dealing with the restoration of Israel, God says, "Behold, I will do a new thing; now it shall spring forth; shall ye not know it? I will even make a way in the wilderness, *and* rivers in the desert" (Isa. 43:19). If God will do a new thing for natural Israel, what about His church, spiritual Israel? Will God not move in ways that are strange to His people so as to catch the attention of the church and cause the church to repent and turn from their wicked ways?

None of us should ever place God in a box. Jonathan

Edwards remonstrated with God's people that no saint should limit the Holy Spirit in His movement. If we limit God then we grieve His Spirit and risk the withdrawal of the Holy Spirit from our presence. There is a danger that we could become lukewarm, having the form of godliness but denying God's power. We must also remember that if there are counterfeit manifestations of the Spirit, then there also must be genuine manifestations.

This chapter, then, is a vindication of the manifestations of the Holy Spirit, especially those other than tongues that have brought concern and controversy. I want to look more closely at the manifestations of "trembling and quaking" and "being slain in the Spirit."

UNDERSTANDING OVERSHADOWING

The title of this chapter, *The Overshadowing of the Spirit,* comes from the early church's view of the manifestations of the Spirit in the world and the church. In particular, the "overshadowing of the Spirit" deals with every manifestation of the Holy Spirit that falls upon the world and the church. It encompasses the very graces of the Holy Spirit in all manners. Further, it includes all the physical manifestations wrought by the Holy Spirit upon individuals, which include trembling, quaking and being slain in the Spirit.

Augustine connected the overshadowing of the Spirit with the incarnation. He also connected it with the promise of the Spirit, power from on high and power that went out of Christ and healed.[4]

John of Damascus connects the overshadowing of the Spirit with doing things that surpass reason and thought. He wrote:

> God said, This is My body, and this is My blood, and this do ye in remembrance of Me. And so it is at His omnipotent command until He come: for it was in this sense that He said until He come: and the overshadowing power of the Holy Spirit becomes through the invocation the rain to this new tillage.

> For just as God made all that He made by the energy
> of the Holy Spirit, so also now the energy of the Spirit
> performs those things that are supernatural and
> which it is not possible to comprehend unless by
> faith alone. "How shall this be," said the holy Virgin,
> "seeing I know not a man?" And the archangel
> Gabriel answered her, "The Holy Spirit shall come
> upon thee, and the power of the Highest shall over-
> shadow thee...The Holy Spirit is present and does
> those things which surpass reason and thought."[5]

Cyril of Jerusalem called it the "overshadowing power
of the Holy Spirit."[6] In dealing with the incarnation, he
joins the overshadowing of the Spirit with the supernatural manifestations of the Holy Spirit and states, "That
overshadowing power of the Highest shall wax wroth."[7]

Tertullian, in dealing with the manifestations of the
Holy Spirit writes:

> For when a man is rapt in the Spirit, especially
> when he beholds the glory of God, or when God
> speaks through him, he necessarily loses his sensa-
> tion and thinking, because he is overshadowed
> with the power of God—a point concerning which
> there is a question between us and the carnally-
> minded.[8]

Tertullian saw that when the Spirit overshadows a
person, he usually loses his senses, his thinking and is
brought forth into a rapture or trance, and becomes as
dead (as the Latin text so indicates by the words *excidat
sensu*). The overshadowing of the Spirit is connected to the
power of God and usually so overwhelms a person that all
sensation, thought, motion and strength disappear. This
often results in a fall to the ground, trembling, quaking
and other such manifestations. Tertullian calls those who
reject the continuation of spiritual gifts and their manifestations as carnally minded.

In commenting upon Matthew 17:1–9, Tertullian
explained that the disciples fell to the ground on their
faces because of the overshadowing of the Spirit. This is

only one dimension of what the overshadowing of the Spirit will do. The early church took this term from Luke 1:35 and Matthew 17:5.

> And the angel answered and said unto her, The Holy Ghost shall come upon thee, and the power of the Highest shall overshadow thee: therefore also that holy thing which shall be born of thee shall be called the Son of God.
>
> —LUKE 1:35

> While he yet spake, behold, a bright cloud overshadowed them: and behold a voice out of the cloud, which said, "This is my beloved Son, in whom I am well pleased; hear ye him."
>
> —MATTHEW 17:5

Being slain in the Spirit is one manifestation of the overshadowing of the Spirit, but the term actually includes other outpourings. Since the overshadowing of the Spirit includes other physical expressions, the trembling and quaking and being slain in the Spirit will be defined separately as parts of this phenomenon.

When the power of God overwhelms the body of a person, the physical body will give way in one manner or another. The body cannot stand the flow of so much energy for very long. As we experience His power, God gives this overflow for many reasons. He refreshes, gives gifts, empowers, anoints, heals, blesses, brings judgment, teaches us, speaks directly to us and has angels speak to us. We may experience this state as lasting seconds, minutes, hours, days or even months.

The genuine experience of being slain in the Spirit does not come about by the anticipation of receiving such a blessing, peer pressure or by trickery. It is a sovereign act of God. We need to be aware that Satan can counterfeit this phenomenon. But we must not dismiss all true manifestations of God just because there are counterfeits. Occultism, occult practices and cults may counterfeit and try to corrupt the manifestations of the Spirit, but God's Spirit is always vindicated.

The phenomenon of being slain in the Spirit can be traced back throughout history to the early church, the writings of the New Testament and the writings of the Old Testament. Opposition to being slain in the Spirit, trembling, shaking and other such manifestations is mostly rooted in the philosophy of John Calvin and the Reformation as previously discussed in chapter two.

The use of catchers for those who are overshadowed by the power of God is not for any purpose other than to protect the church or minister from being sued. Some could pretend to fall under the power and claim that they have been hurt so that they can bring a lawsuit against the church or minister. In the genuine overshadowing of the Spirit, most never become hurt if the person comes in submission under the power of God. However, it is possible for a person to come up for prayer, being in submission under the power of God, and God knocks that person down so hard that it causes harm. This is a sovereign act of God in the realm of grace to show His might, His power and His reality to the person, congregation, people or minister. The harm will be healed or undone as soon as God has finished His work. Further, it is more than possible that if a person comes in arrogance with a wrong motive or an unwillingness to submit to God's power and will that he will be knocked down as a sign of discipline. In these cases, God is proving His sovereignty and also proving a point, as seen in Saint Paul's case. (See Acts 9.) God may come in the overshadowing as a lamb with gentleness or as a lion with power, fury and anger.

There are three reasons why a person may not succumb to these physical manifestations of the Spirit. There may be a lack of faith or a lack of surrender to the Spirit. God may also desire to touch the individual in a different way. In this case, the Spirit desires to work veiled and quietly. It may be that the person is fearful of these manifestations, and the Holy Spirit will work in such a manner to show the person that what is happening is truly from Him.

The term "trembling and quaking" in the biblical context denotes that the power of the Holy Spirit has overshadowed

the body of a person so greatly that he shakes uncontrollably, as the manifestation of these effects. It is positive
proof that God is Creator of the bodies, lives and minds of
the individuals.

"Being slain in the Spirit" is the effect on the body by the
power of the Holy Spirit whereby the body loses its
strength, causing the person to fall. It is common for those
who receive this blessing to lose feeling or control. It may
also be defined as "the total loss of all motor control over
the body." It may include the person falling into a trance
while beholding visions, hearing the voice of God and
angels. This phenomenon also includes tongues being
spoken, laughing, weeping or praising God. Accompanying
these physical manifestations will be other spiritual and
mental manifestations.

This next section is divided into two parts. The first part
will deal with providing scriptural proof that both trembling and quaking as well as being slain in the Spirit
occurred in Old and New Testament times. Quotations or
endnotes are given for further enlightenment. The second
part deals with the history of these types of manifestations.

SCRIPTURAL EVIDENCE

In Luke 1:35, Mary is overshadowed by the Holy Spirit for
the purpose of the incarnation. Notice, however, that the
overshadowing includes more than the incarnation.
Though this was the primary reason and purpose, it was
also used to empower Mary, to give her strength and to
refine her for what she would have to endure. Further, the
overshadowing had physical effects upon her person other
than the incarnation of God the Word. The Greek verb
ἐπίσκιάζω (ĕpēskēäzō) is used in the indicative and future
tense. The meaning of this Greek verb is more comprehensive than once thought. The verb takes upon itself the
idea of the Holy Spirit's power overshadowing Mary. It
suggests that this power overcomes and overwhelms her.
She becomes weakened by its presence and becomes as
dead. According to the thought of the Greek text, such an
overshadowing would produce the same effects that the

disciples experienced in Matthew 17:6 as well as other places in the Old and New Testaments. Mary trembled, quaked, lost her strength and fell down to the ground. In essence, the power of this Greek verb contrasts her finiteness with God's infiniteness. It emphasizes her weakness and God's power. It highlights her total surrender to God. God wanted her to be motionless and totally surrender to Him so that He could work unhindered.

The power of this Greek verb discredits those who are skeptical of manifestations of the Holy Spirit. Gnosticism taught that all things which are of the body or which deal with the body are evil. Skeptics follow this same philosophy about the physical manifestations wrought by the Holy Spirit upon the bodies of individuals.

The early church connected ἐπίσκιάζω with the glory of the tabernacle and the divine presence residing in the temple. They saw that the overshadowing of the Spirit was the tabernacling or indwelling of the Spirit in the church so much so that it overwhelmed individuals and caused many manifestations. The overshadowing of the Spirit also took place when healing occurred in the ministry of Christ.

From the Greek Septuagint, the Greek verb ἐπίσκιάζω is connected to the Shekinah glory as related in Exodus 40:35, where the cloud of glory rested in the tent of the congregation. So strong was the presence of the Lord that Moses could not enter. Such was God's presence that no one could stand in such awesome power.

In John 18:6, the word of Christ was so filled with the power of the Holy Spirit that the band of men and officers (numbering six hundred) who were present to arrest Christ fell backward to the ground. This is another example of the overshadowing of the Spirit. Though Christ retained His divine power, He refused to use it. (See Philippians 2:5–7.) Christ was endowed with the power of the Holy Spirit. (See Philippians 2:6–7; Hebrews 2:14–18; 5:8–9; Isaiah 7:14–16; 11:1; 50:4–11; 53:1–12; Luke 3:21–22; Acts 10:38.) The power of the Holy Spirit that flowed out of the mouth of Christ overwhelmed the people so that they fell backward.

The interpretation of the Greek text leaves no doubt that the people fell under the power of the Holy Spirit, succumbing to it physically and falling down to the ground. According to the Greek text, the people immediately fell backward. A force of such awesome power touched their bodies that they succumbed to its power and strength. They were weakened by its energy and fell as dead. The Greek verb πίπτω (pēptō) denotes that people fell unintentionally by something other than their own means or power. A power not their own overwhelmed their bodies, and they fell out because of that power.

This same Greek verb indicates that being slain in the Spirit is a form of prostration before the Lord. Prostration is a sign that we are aware of the overwhelming awe and supernatural power of God to the extreme. (See Daniel 10:9.) It is also a sign of humility, respect, reverence and the proper attitude for those receiving an immediate revelation from God. (See Genesis 17:3; 18:2; 19:1; Ruth 2:10; Ezekiel 1:28; 3:23; 43:4; 44:4; Matthew 17:6; 28:4; Acts 9:4–9; 16:29; Revelation 1:17; 4–5; 19:10; 22:8; 1 Samuel 25:33; 28:14.) This positioning may be done intentionally or unintentionally, by the power of God or through the power of the person in question.

The awesome presence of the Lord struck such weakness and fear in the disciples that it resulted in them falling upon their faces. (See Matthew 17:5.) The Holy Spirit's overshadowing took the form of a cloud in this passage. In Matthew 28:4, the presence of the Lord was so strong that two keepers shook and became like dead.

The Greek phrase "ἀπὸ δέ τοῦ φόβου" (äpō thĕ tou phōvou) is known in Greek grammar as the *genitive of cause* and the *ablative of source*. These constructions show that fear was the source of the shaking and falling down to the ground that the men experienced. The source of the fear was the power of God overshadowing the keepers through the angel's presence.

Though some deny that this incident is an example of being slain in the Spirit, the Greek shows the opposite. The power of God shone forth through the angel and brought forth fear as well as other emotional and physical manifestations upon those who were present.

The Greek verb σείω (sēō) indicates two important things. First, the shaking was not done willingly or intentionally. Something outside of the keepers was pushing and pressing forward to cause this effect. In a full range of thought, this Greek verb indicates that the keepers were mentally, spiritually and physically shaking. Their whole beings were under this pressure of power. Second, the aorist tense is found in what is known as the *comprehensive aorist*. This type of aorist shows that the shaking went on for some time. It was severe in its effect and left a lasting impression upon the keepers.

The Greek verb γίνομαι (yēnōmĕ), connected to the Greek phrase "ὡς νεκροί" (ōs nĕkrē) in its structure, informs the reader that a miracle is taking place. The fact that the keepers fell down and became lifeless was in fact a miracle. This event is connected to the gift of working of miracles. It also conveys that the keepers entered into a new state of existence for a time where all sensation ceased and they lost all motor control over their bodies.

The overshadowing of the Spirit is clearly seen in the experiences of Paul. In Acts 9:3–4 the light of the Lord overshadowed Paul (Saul). This light was a manifestation of the power of the Spirit and was much more than a light. It was the Shekinah glory and the divine power manifested toward and around Paul. It affected him so much that he lost his strength and fell to the ground. He was weakened by such an awesome manifestation of God's power.

The Greek verb πίπτω (pēptō) literally says that a force beyond Paul's imagination fell upon his body so that his body fell down to the ground. The verb is written as a present participle, which indicates that when Paul was falling to the ground under the shadow of the Spirit, he heard the voice of the Lord. Acts 9:4 and Acts 26:14 in the Greek mean the same.

Ezekiel was so overwhelmed by the Shekinah glory that he fell forward upon his face. (See Ezekiel 1:28.) Paul and the keepers fell in the sense of collapsing under the power of the Spirit. Others have fallen backward. (See John 18:6.)

The significance of the direction of the fall is undeniable. Those who fall forward signify the Old Testament saints looking toward the cross. Those who fall backward signify the New Testament saints looking backward to the cross. Those who collapse signify that all the saints must stay beneath the cross and reside under its protection.

Daniel reels under the power of the revelations and the overshadowing of the Spirit. (See Daniel 7:28.) He was also in a deep sleep with his face toward the ground by the same overshadowing of the Spirit brought on through the angel. (See Daniel 8:18.) The same thing occurred to Daniel in Daniel 10:6–7. In this passage, Daniel retained no strength. That is what the power of God can do to those who come into contact with it. The weakness is the result of the overshadowing of the Spirit.

The Hebrew verb רָדַם (rädäm) in this passage carries the notion that Daniel had fallen on his face, unconscious and lifeless. This same verb is a powerful signal as to the full effect of the Spirit upon Daniel. It shows that a person can literally lose consciousness and all sensation and be seen as dead. The power that this verb conveys is firm proof of this miraculous occurrence brought about by the Spirit. Furthermore, this same verb is the equivalent of the Greek verb πίπτω (pēptō) in thought. This Greek verb gives in most cases the same patterns and range of thought. Thus in the New Testament the examples given can well include a loss of consciousness, sensation and being frozen to the ground.

Notice that a great quaking fell upon the men who did not see the vision. Actually what fell upon them was fear. But the fear in turn caused physical trembling and quaking. This is seen by the Hebrew and Greek nouns used.

Moses said, "I exceedingly fear and tremble" (Hebrews 12:21). The trembling was due to the awesome sight of God's power. Acts 7:32 reads:

> Saying, I am the God of thy fathers, the God of Abraham, and the God of Isaac, and the God of Jacob. Then Moses trembled, and durst not behold.

In Ezra 9:4, the very words of God bring forth the physical manifestation of trembling. This passage reads:

> Then were assembled unto me every one that trembled at the words of the God of Israel, because of the transgression of those that had been carried away; and I sat astonished until the evening sacrifice.

Habakkuk also relates that he trembled. (See Habakkuk 3:16.) Other examples of people trembling under the presence of God for one reason or another are found in Psalms 119:120 and Acts 19:26.

In 2 Chronicles 5:14, it is said that the Shekinah glory filled the whole house of God so much that the priests could not stand to minister. What is that, but falling out by the overshadowing of the Spirit? The priests, it is recorded, could not stand the blazing power of God and became weakened and unable to stand. They were unable to minister as priests because their job required them to stand and give offerings.

John the Apostle experienced the overshadowing of the Spirit in Revelation 1:17 where he "fell at his feet as dead." The phrase "fell at his feet as dead" delivers such a sense of God's grace and power as it affects the senses, mind and body of John that it cannot be easily denied. Indeed, this phrase powerfully presents the full effect of the overshadowing upon John. The loss of consciousness, sensation and motor controls of the body caused John to be frozen to the ground as though dead.

HISTORICAL EVIDENCE

In the midst of so much knowledge about the Word of God and the history of the church, the modern church seems ignorant of both. The church today has forgotten where they have come from. We have denied our blessings, our heritage and all those who have gone before us. In essence, the saints of today have robbed themselves of the glories and blessings of the church of yesterday. Many have closed their minds and their willingness to run back to the experiences of the early church.

Tertullian mentions two martyrs, Perpetua and Felicitas, in his writings. The woman Perpetua was said to have been so deeply in the Spirit and in ecstasy that she aroused as if from sleep. Tertullian writes:

> Then Perpetua was received by a certain one who was still a catechumen, Rusticus by name, who kept close to her; and she, as if aroused from sleep, so deeply had she been in the Spirit and in an ecstasy, began to look round her, and to say to the amazement of all, "I cannot tell when we are to be led out to that cow." And when she had heard what had already happened, she did not believe it until she had perceived certain signs of injury in her body and in her dress, and had recognized the catechumen. Afterwards causing that catechumen and the brother to approach, she addressed them, saying, "Stand fast in the faith, and love one another, all of you, and be not offended at my sufferings."[9]

Here in this example, Tertullian states that the catechumen, Rusticus, kept close to Perpetua. Undoubtedly, he was there, as a catcher, to catch her if she fell out. The description of falling out under the power of the Holy Spirit was "as if aroused from sleep." In several instances, the overshadowing of the Spirit is portrayed as sleep. Perpetua had been so under the power of God that she did not know what had happened to her. God's mercy and grace allowed Perpetua to experience this so that she could withstand her death as a martyr. What a way to meet God!

In the early church, the phrase "as if asleep" and other similar phrases dealt with the overshadowing of the Spirit and, in particular, being slain in the Spirit as part of this overshadowing.

Augustine, denying at one time the manifestations of the Holy Spirit, experienced face to face the awesome power of the Holy Spirit in his city of Hippo. One particular miracle occurred to a young man named Paulus. He had been cursed with a hideous shaking in all his limbs that his six brothers and two sisters also suffered from. Paulus and his sister Palladia came to a church before Easter to pray that God might restore their health. On Sunday, something wonderful took place in their lives. Augustine relates:

> In the morning, when there was now a large crowd present, and the young man was holding the bars of the holy place where the relics were, and praying, suddenly he fell down, and lay precisely as if asleep, but not trembling as he was wont to do even in sleep. All present were astonished. Some were alarmed, some were moved with pity, and while some were for lifting him up, others prevented them, and said they should rather wait and see what would result. And behold! He rose up, and trembled no more, for he was healed, and stood quite well, scanning those who were scanning him...The whole church was filled with the voices of those who were shouting and congratulating him...The young woman when she had come down from the steps where she had been standing, went to pray at the holy relics, and no sooner had she touched the bars than she, in the same way as her brother, collapsed, as if falling asleep, and rose up cured.[10]

In the Gospel of Nicodemus, it is recorded that Joseph of Arimathaea spoke to the rulers of the Synagogue, the priests and the Levites. When these men heard the words of Joseph, such power overshadowed them that they became as dead and fell to the ground. Then Nicodemus and Joseph exhorted all of them to rise up, stand upon their feet and strengthen their lives. The power of God overwhelmed their whole beings and they succumbed to that power.[11]

In the book entitled *Life and Conduct of the Holy Women Xanthippe, Polyxena, and Rebecca*, Xanthippe "was overcome by an unspeakable joy and fell to the ground." It is said that Polyxena held Xanthippe, waiting for this movement of God to end.[12] In another section of this book, Xanthippe was overcome again with the power of the Spirit, but this time through an angel.[13]

In the work known as *Recognitions of Clement,* it is written:

> But as soon as Peter pronounced our names, all the old man's limbs were weakened, and he fell down in a swoon. But we his sons rushed to him, and embraced and kissed him, fearing that we might not be able to recall his spirit... But Peter ordered us to rise from embracing our father, lest we should kill him, and he himself laying hold of his hand, and lifting him up as from a deep sleep, and gradually reviving him.[14]

In this example, an old man fell out, so totally overwhelmed by the power of the Holy Spirit, that he was weakened and swooned and fainted. He was so under the power of the Holy Spirit that he was frozen to the ground and Peter had to gradually revive him. What a miracle and an awesome act of God!

In the Gospel of Nicodemus, Joseph experienced something wonderful after the resurrection of Jesus. Jesus Himself appeared to him after He had risen from the grave. Joseph not only was slain in the Spirit but even experienced the trembling caused by the power of the Spirit.

The Gospel reads:

> And when midnight came, as I was standing and praying, the house where you shut me in was hung up by the four corners, and there was a flashing of light in mine eyes. And I fell to the ground trembling. Then someone lighted me up from the place where I had fallen and poured over me an abundance of water from the head even to the feet, and put round my nostrils the odor of a wonderful ointment, and rubbed my face with the water itself, as if washing me, and kissed me, and said to me, "Joseph fear not, but open thine eyes and see who it is that speaks to thee." And looking, "I saw Jesus."[15]

In the work entitled the *Pastor of Hermas*, Hermas was seized with trembling and quaking all over his body.[16] In other books it is reported that Mary, under the overshadowing of the Spirit, was trembling and quaking quite a lot.[17] Another work describes that Pilate fell under the overshadowing of the Spirit so much that he trembled greatly.[18] In another work, Jesus appears to many people after He had risen from the grave. Many were seized with trembling.[19]

It is a known fact that the overshadowing of the Spirit occurred before and after the time of Jonathan Edwards and John Wesley. People like Moody, Finney, Peter Cartwright, and in particular Maria B. Woodworth-Etter, beheld this phenomenon. It was reported in the *St. Louis Post-Dispatch* that many people had experienced this phenomenon in Woodworth-Etter's revival. It was this phenomenon that characterized her meetings more than anything else. In one particular event, so many people fell under the power of God that Mrs. Woodworth-Etter was frightened. She had never seen anything like this. However, the Lord had already told her in a vision that this would take place. In that one incident, people were seen as dead, and after two hours they all, one after the other, "sprang to their feet as quick as a flash, with shining faces, and shouted all over the house."[20]

In the Revival at Cane Ridge Kentucky in 1801, which was part of the Second Great Awakening, so many people were slain in the Spirit that the field was covered with hundreds of bodies. It looked like a battle had been fought.

It was reported that the great preacher, Mr. Bolton, who was born in 1572, fell under the power of God and lay on the ground. All those present were struck with awe and fear at the awesome power of God. It was reported that the body of Mr. Bolton seemed as dead, that neither speech, sense, blood, nor heat appeared in him. He remained this way for months. Afterward, he recovered with no apparent harm. It was as if his body had been in a state of suspended animation.[21]

What has almost escaped the thinking of people is the

fact that Martin Luther was also overshadowed with the Spirit in the same fashion as Bolton. Martin Luther fell out under the power and remained this way for up to twenty-four hours.

The great preacher Rothwell, who lived in the seventeenth century, said that when he preached the Word of God people trembled under the power of God. This occurred in every meeting of his for years.[22]

Also in the seventeenth century, Mr. Blackerby was so filled with God's power that when people entered into his very presence they would tremble under the hand of God. [23]

Countless other examples of this phenomenon could well be given. The examples laid out here are far more than any other book has given. One example of God working in a particular manner is sufficient for both critics and proof that God is doing now what was done in the past. I have tried to provide examples throughout Old and New Testament history to illustrate the effects of the power of God. Studying the past helps us know where we are in our present and where we will be in the future.

A writer once wrote, "Men plan; God laughs." We often believe that we have figured out God. We may have concluded that God will only move in this way or that. When men do this, God laughs. It must be understood that God's Spirit has His own rules and patterns. The Spirit moves as He sees fit, not as men believe or think. Consequently, the physical manifestations of the Spirit are within the rules and guidelines of the Holy Spirit. These physical effects that the Holy Spirit brings upon the bodies of individuals are perfectly sound, holy and biblical. Let us stop judging by our eyes and begin judging by the Word, which will always be in agreement with the Spirit. (See 1 John 5:5–10; Galatians 1:8.)

NOTES

CHAPTER ONE
Scriptural Evidence for the Gifts

1. *Disputation with Manes*, 37; *Origen Against Celsus*, 6:19–22.

2. *Banquet of the Ten Virgins*, 9:1–4.

3. *Of Patience*, 12–14.

4. Genesis 1–3; 5:24; 6:2; 6:9–8:19; 11:1; 12:1–3, 17; 15:12–21; 16:7; 17:1; 18:1; 19:11, 23, 26; 20:3, 17; 21:1; 22:11; 24:12; 25:21, 23; 26:2, 24; 28:12; 31:3; 32:1, 24; 35:9; 37:5; 38:7; 40:1; 41:1; 1 Kings 3:3; 8:10; 11:29; 13:1, 20; 14:5; 16:1; 2 Kings 15:5; 19:20, 35; 20:5, 10, 16; 21:10; 22:14; 2 Chronicles 7:1; 11:2; Ezra 5:1; Job 1–2; Daniel 2:1; 3:1; 4:19–28; 5:5, 17; 6:1; 7–12.

5. 1 Peter 2:24; 3:14–21; Matthew 5:48; 8:17; Isaiah 53; Romans 2:4; 6:1–23; 8:11; 10:9; John 3:16, 36; 5:24; 6:40, 47; 8:51; 11:26; Mark 16:16; Acts 2:38; 14:7; Revelation 2:11; 20:6, 11–15; 1 John 5:12; Hebrews 6:17–19; 2 Timothy 2:13; Psalm 18:30; 45:4; 91:4; Deuteronomy 32:4; 33:21.

6. Hebrews 2:14–15; 9:26; 1 Corinthians 6:19; 15:51–58; Matthew 20:28; 1 Peter 1:18; 2:24; 4:12–13; 1 Timothy 2:6; Romans 3:25; 5:10; 1 John 2:2; 2 Corinthians 5:18; John 9:1–4; 11:4; 12:31–32; Ephesians 1:7; Exodus 4:11; Revelation 11:16; 16:1; 20:7–10, 13–14; Job 2:7; 7:5, 13–15; 16:8; 19:17; 23:10; 30:17; Luke 1:9–20; Acts 5:5–10; 12:23; 13:11; Isaiah 2:2–4; 33:24; 53:6–12; 65:17; Jeremiah 30:17; Ezekiel 34:16.

7. Acts 2; 3:1; 8:18; 9:10–18; 10:45–46; 11:28; 13:32; 14:4–14; 19:6; 21:4, 9; 21:10–11; Galatians 1:19; 1 Corinthians 15:7; 16:19; Romans 16:7; Acts 18:2, 18, 26; Romans 16:3; 2 Timothy 4:19.

8. *Church History of Eusebius*, 7:7.

CHAPTER TWO
Historical Evidence for the Gifts

1. "A Sermon on Keeping Children in School," *Luther's Works*, 46:224.

2. John Foxe, *The Acts and Monuments, in Eight Volumes*, 4:319.

3. John Luther, *The Works of John Luther*, 31:115.

4. *Calvin's Institutes of the Christian Religion*, 1:271.

5. John Foxe, op. cit., 4:253.

6. Ibid., 4:254.

7. Ibid., 4:255.

8. John Gillies, *Historical Collections of Accounts of Revival*, 29.

9. John Foxe, op. cit., 4:256.

10. Ibid., 4:256.

11. Ibid., 4:259.

12. Ibid., 3:447.

13. *Tertullian Against Marcion*, 5:15.

14. Ibid., Apology 23.

15. *Apology*, 22–24; *To Scapula*, 2–5; *Soul's Testimony*, 2–4; *Octavius of Minucius Felix*, 27–29.

16. *Treatise on the Soul*, 9–11.

17. *Tertullian Against Marcion*, 5:8; *Perpetua and Pelicitas, Preface*, 1; *Irenæus Against Heresies*, 5:5–7; *Constitutions of the Holy Apostles*, 2:8.

18. *On Fasting*, 1–2.

19. *Constitutions of the Holy Apostles*, 8:1–2.

20. Augustine, *On the Trinity*, 15, 26.

21. *The Gospel of Thomas*, 12.

22. *Epistle of Ignatius to the Philippians*, 2.

23. *Epistle of Ignatius to the Philadelphians*, 7–9.

24. *Dialogue with Trypho*, 82–87; 29–32; *Second Apology of Justin*, 5–8.

25. *Irenæus Against Heresies*, 2:31–33; 1:13.

26. Ibid.,5:5–7.

27. Ibid., 4:9–11.

28. *Epistles of Cyprian*, 74:10–15.

29. *Epistles of Cyprian*, 74; 75–76; *Treatises of Cyprian*, 5.

30. *Epistles of Cyprian*, 10–11.

31. Ibid., 1–2.

32. *The Pastor of Hermas*, 2:12, 2–6; 3:9, 14–17.

33. Ibid., 11

34. Michael Green, *Evangelism in the Early Church*, 201–202.

35. *Tertullian Against Praxeas* 1; *On Fasting*, 1–2.

36. *Origen Against Celsus*, 1:1–2; 3:24–26; 7:4–8; 7:68–70.

37. Appendix to the *Works of Hippolytus; Heads of Canons.*

38. *Arnobius Against the Heathen*, 1:46–49.

39. John Foxe, op. cit., 3:73.

40. Ibid., 3:73.

41. *Two Epistles Concerning Virginity*, 11–13.

42. John L. Sherrill, *They Speak With Other Tongues*, 76.

43. Lecture, 1; Lecture 17.

44. Letter 22.

45. *De Trinitate*, 11: 1–7.

46. *On the Spirit*, 29:74–75.

47. *Ecclesiastical History*, 28.

48. *Church History of Eusebius*, 3:5–6:10; 7:1–10.

49. *Life of Constantine*, 1:27–33.

50. *Church History of Eusebius*, 8:9–11.

51. Athanasius, Letter 49.

52. *Life of Antony*, 36–50.

53. Ibid., 50–67.

54. *On Care to Be Had for the Dead*, 19–22.

55. *Letters of Augustine*, 78; *On Epistle of John*, Homily 6.

56. *On John*, 13; *On John*, 32; *On Epistle of John*, Homily 6.

57. John L. Sherrill, op. cit., 76.

58. *On John*, 26.

59. *Cassian's Conferences, Second Conference of Abbot Nesteros, On Divine Gifts.*

60. *Institutes of John Cassian*, 4:23.

61. Sulpitius Severus, *On The Life of St. Martin*, Preface, 1–27.

62. *Dialogues of Sulpitius Severus*, 1:26.

63. *Ecclesiastical History of Sozomen*, 7:22–24.

64. Ibid., 6:28–29.

65. *Ecclesiastical History of Socrates Scholasticus*, 4:23–24.

66. Ibid., 4:23–25.

67. Ibid., 1:18–20.

68. John L. Sherrill, op. cit., 76–78.

69. H. A. Baker, *Visions Beyond the Veil*, 1–122.

70. Christian History, *Revival at Cane Ridge*, 10–15.

71. John Wesley, *The Works of John Wesley*, 10:56.

72. Ibid., 92–120.

73. Ibid., 533.

74. Ibid., 131.

75. Ibid., 10:23.

76. Ibid., 108.

77. Ibid., 110.

78. Ibid., 110–111.

79. Jonathan Edwards, *The Works of Jonathan Edwards*, 1:234–343, 266, 368–370, 375–376.

80. Ibid., 1:375.

81. Ibid., 1:375.

82. Ibid., 2:261.

83. Ibid., 2:262, 270.

84. Ibid., 2:274–275.

CHAPTER THREE
The Overshadowing of the Spirit

1. Augustine, *The City of God*, Book 22, 10.

2. Jonathan Edwards, *The Works of Jonathan Edwards*, 2:261.

3. Ibid., 2:261.

4. Augustine, *On the Gospel of John*, Tractate XCIX.

5. John of Damascus, *An Exact Exposition of the Orthodox Faith*, 4:13.

6. Cyril of Jerusalem, *Catechetical Lectures*, 12.

7. Ibid., 12.

8. Tertullian, *The Five Books Against Marcion*, 4:22.

9. Ibid., *The Passion of the Holy Martyrs Perpetua and Felicitas.*

10. Augustine, *The City of God*, Book 22, 8.

11. *The Gospel of Nicodemus*, 16.

12. *The Life and Conduct of the Holy Women Xanthippe, Polyxena, and Rebecca*, 41.

13. Ibid., 15.

14. *Recognitions of Clement*, 35–36.

15. *The Gospel of Nicodemus*, Latin form, 15.

16. *Pastor of Hermas, Third Vision*, 1.

17. *The Gospel of Pseudo-Matthew*, 2.

18. *The Report of Pilate Procurator.*

19. *The Narrative of Joseph*, 4.

20. Maria Woodworth-Etter, *A Diary of Signs and Wonders*, 37.

21. John Gillies, *Historical Collections of Accounts of Revival*, 87.

22. Ibid., 85.

23. Ibid., 112.

GLOSSARY

A

Ablative of source—A grammatical construction that states the source of someone or something.

Agabus—A Christian prophet of the first century A.D. The Lord sent Agabus to Paul in 44 A.D. and predicted a famine. Some years later, Agabus gave Paul a prophetic word.

Alogianism—A sect of unorthodox Christians that believed and taught several heresies and blasphemies during the second century. Some of the heresies and blasphemies included denying the deity of Christ, denying the Trinity, denying the Gospel of John, and denying the continuation of the gifts and their manifestations. This sect followed very closely the teachings of the Gnostics.

Ambrose (344–397) —A bishop and theologian in the fourth century. In 370 A.D., he became bishop of Milan. He is numbered among the four great Latin theologians, with Augustine, Jerome and Gregory the Great.

Ananias—A Christian who lived in Damascus. He baptized Saul and was welcomed into the community of Christians.

Andronicus—He was one of the seventy apostles and became bishop of Fannonia. In Acts 16:7, Paul, as a fellow apostle, honors Andronicus. Andronicus was older in the Lord than Paul and became someone that Paul depended upon to help him in the endeavors of the Lord.

Anointing—The anointing is the position and rank of a Christian along with the power necessary to hold that position and rank. With this, it further comprises the gifts of the Holy Spirit as well as the Holy Spirit Himself from whom flows all the gifts, powers and graces of the saints and who is typified in several passages. (See 1 John 2:20; Exodus 28:41; 29:7, 29; 30:25, 30.)

Antony, Saint (251–356)—A hermit who was used by the Lord in spiritual gifts and their manifestations.

Apostles—The word *apostle* means "one who is sent or a missionary." This was understood by the disciples of Christ who were commissioned to go to the nations for Christ's sake as missionaries, preaching Christ's message of redemption, including

Matthias, the seventy disciples and a host of others. (See Matthew 28:18–20; Acts 1:21–26; Luke 10:1.)

Apostolic age—The age that comprised the lives of the twelve apostles ending unofficially in 100 A.D., but officially at the death of John the Apostle in 96 A.D. In other words, the apostolic age is the first period in the history of Christianity, ending with the death of the last of the twelve apostles.

Aquila—One of the seventy apostles, and one of Paul's closest friends and coworkers at spreading the unalterable Gospel of Christ.

Archelaus—A bishop of the early church who wrote against a heretic sect. His work, *The Acts of the Disputation with the Heresiarch Manes*, was written in 277 A.D. Very little is known about him, and very little remains of his work.

Arnobius (d. 330 A.D.)—A Christian theologian and father of the early church who lived during the time of the Roman emperor Diocletian (284–305). His greatest work, *Adversus Nationes*, is a defense of Christianity against the systems and practices of the pagans.

Ascetic movement—This movement swept through the church in Egypt and Asia Minor and continued very strongly until the ninth century. For the first three hundred years of the church, this movement's purpose was the preparation of Christians for martyrdom and to teach Christians to remain virgins. Further, the movement stressed self-denial, renunciation of all earthly possessions, fasting, and perpetual virginity. This lead to a life shut off from the world in monasteries where men became monks, and in later times, women became nuns.

Athanasius (293–373)—A Christian theologian, father and bishop of Alexandria. When the early church was turning away from the path of orthodoxy in the fourth century, Athanasius stood against the struggle wrought upon the church by Arius who denied the deity of Christ and said that Christ was a creature, not equal to God, but of like substance with the Father. He was the main opponent of Arius and helped to bring the debate over Christ to the forefront.

Atheism—A system of belief, which in reality is a religion among its own right, that denies the existence of any deity, not only the pagan gods, but the God of the Scriptures as well. It places man as the center of the universe and sets man as ever increasing and moving toward an exalted state of evolution where man may be considered as a god.

Augustine (354–430)—The greatest father of the Latin Church and one of the most eminent Western fathers of the church. Before his conversion, Augustine followed several pagan philosophies. The most influential pagan philosophy upon his life was known as Manichaeism. Manichaeism taught a Persian dualistic philosophy where two eternal forces, one good and one evil, are in absolute conflict against each other. Manichaeism denied free will. The foundation of Augustine's view about election and predestination is found in Manichaeism. Even with this, Augustine was considered a great theologian, a defender of orthodoxy and a great scholar.

Barnabas—An apostle who was one of the members of the early church in Jerusalem, and he was a companion of Paul.

Basil (329–379)—A father and theologian of the church. He was the patriarch of Eastern monasticism. Basil, his brother St. Gregory of Nyssa, and their friend St. Gregory of Nazianzus were three defenders of orthodoxy.

Beelzebub—Another name for Satan.

Blackerby—A seventeenth-century revivalist, theologian and minister who experienced the awesome power of God firsthand.

Bolton—A seventeenth-century revivalist, theologian and minister.

C

Calvin, John (1509–1564)—A French reformer and founder of a system of doctrine known as Calvinism. His system of doctrine was derived and founded upon Augustinianism.

Cassian, John (d. 433)—A writer on asceticism, a theologian and father of the early church.

Christ—The term *Christ* means "anointed one" or "anointing." It has precise reference to the Messiah long foretold. Christ came to this world, became man, was born of a virgin, shed his blood on the cross as a substitutionary atonement for the sins of the world, was buried, descended into the underworld as a Conqueror, rose bodily and ascended to the right hand of the

Father. He is the Redeemer, Savior, Son of God, God the Word, God the Son, and Messiah.

Christianity—In its true form and essence, it is the very relationship between God and man wrought by the death of Christ Jesus. Christianity may also be defined as the doctrine of salvation, delivered to man by Christ Jesus, the Son of God, who assuming our nature of a pure virgin, taught the Jews the true way to happiness, confirming His message by miracles.

Chrysostom (349–407)—A theologian and father of the early church. He was considered one of the greatest early Christian orators of preaching. He wrote many works including homilies, epistles, treatises and liturgies.

Cistercian movement—The Cistercians were a Roman Catholic monastic order founded in 1098 in France by a group of Benedictine monks. Their purpose was to establish a community that would strictly follow the monastic rules established by St. Benedict. The growth of this movement was great. By 1153, there were more than three hundred Cistercian monasteries. By the end of the Middle Ages, there were more than seven hundred Cistercian abbeys. Their most influential time was that of the twelfth century.

City of Nisibis—A city of Mesopotamia, situated on the Mygdonius River at the foot of Mt. Masius.

Constantine the Great (274–337)—The first Roman emperor who converted to Christianity.

Cornelius—The first Gentile to be converted. He was a Roman centurion in the Italian cohort stationed at Caesare. (See Acts 10.)

Customary present—This type of present tense represents action as repeatedly occurring on a habitual or regular basis or an action that can be expected to happen.

Cyprian (200–258)—A theologian and father of the early church, the leader of the Christian church in Africa who became the bishop of Carthage. He became a martyr of the Lord when Cyprian was tried and was murdered by beheading.

Cyril of Alexandria (380–444)—A bishop and theologian at Alexandria. His great hour in his Christian faith was his defense of the unity of Christ's person, divine and human, against the teaching of Nestorius.

De Clum, John—A Bohemian reformer and friend of John Huss.

Deliverances—Acts of grace where the people who are oppressed and possessed of evil are set free from the power, influence, dominion and effects of Satan and his forces.

Demons—Evil creatures who have, through free will, allied themselves with Satan to kill, steal, destroy and bring whatever ills they can upon the human race. They have also conspired to destroy God, His angels and His eternal plan.

Denominations—The various sects of Christianity.

Didache—A written document in which the oral teachings of the apostles have come down to the church. Its date of composition ranges from the first century to the third century.

Dionysius (190–265)—A bishop of Alexandria and a powerful Christian theologian.

Dispensationalism—A system of Bible interpretation that traces back, in one form or another, to the early church and the Jewish scholars. The system recognizes that different times mean different things in the Bible. It works to interpret the Word of God according to the time that each part of the Bible deals with. Dispensationalism shows that the Word of God is to be divided into several dispensations, and in each dispensation God deals differently with the His creatures.

Divine presence—It is the Shekinah presence, which is a visible and invisible divine manifestation of God's glory, though not full or complete, accompanied with one or more of the following elements: fire or a pillar of fire, light, brightness, mist, thick darkness, clouds, lightning, thunderstorm, the voice of the Lord, the appearance of the Lord, the appearance of an angel, and/or the Lord's power.

Є

Early church—The church in its first three centuries. It may also denote the period from the first century to the eighth or ninth century.

Edwards, Jonathan (1703–1758)—A revivalist and theologian firmly set in the history of New England Calvinism and the "Great Awakening" revival.

Emotionalism—A state of being prompted by emotion and feelings, not by the power of God.

Epaphroditus—A Christian believer from Philippi. He became a companion of Paul. (See Philippians 2:25.)

Ephraem (306–373)—A biblical and ecclesiastical writer. He is also known as a theologian and poet. He wrote many songs and articles against false doctrines.

Eusebius of Caesarea (265–339)—A historian of the early church. He was the founder of the theological school of Caesarea and became the bishop of Caesarea about 314. His greatest contribution to Christianity was his work on the history of the church.

Fanaticism—A state of being prompted not by facts or by evidences, but by irrational thinking that greatly exceeds the norm in beliefs, actions, morals and doctrines, as pertaining to the Christian faith.

Franciscan movement—A movement began as a religious order founded in 1208 by Saint Francis of Assisi. It was given approval by Pope Innocent III in 1209. The Franciscans have been known for their devotion to learning, and they held many positions in universities before the Reformation. A group of Franciscans accompanied Christopher Columbus on his first voyage to the New World.

Full gospel—The gospel in which the Spirit and Word are united together in perfect unity.

Genitive of cause—It is that which states the cause of someone or something.

Gifts, spiritual—The manifestations and endowments of the Holy Spirit that enter into the reality of the believer, the church and the world. (See 1 Corinthians 12:7.)

Gnosticism—The belief and religious system that exalts knowledge and revelation over grace and faith as the key to one's salvation and incorporates many philosophies into itself, exalting heathenism above all. Gnosticism consists of Oriental mysticism, Greek philosophy, Platonistic, Cabalistic Judaism and other heathen philosophies combined with a perverted Christian thought.

Gospel—The good news of redemption.

Gospel of Nicodemus—A New Testament work of the Apocrypha written between the third and fifth centuries.

Great Awakening—A series of revivals in the American colonies between 1725 and 1760.

Gregory of Nyssa (330–395)—A bishop of Nyssa. He was considered a Cappadocian father and younger brother of Basil. Both were defenders of the plurality of persons within the Godhead.

Healings—Acts of God's grace whereby the physical body is restored and made whole again through the power of God. They may be simple healings, which are done gradually, or miraculous healings, which are done instantaneously. Miraculous healings are miracles, signs and wonders while simple healings may only be seen as sign and wonders. Healings, in this work, center on the physical healings of the body, but healings in general may also be mental and emotional. The gifts of healings do not just deal with physical healings, but are present for the banishment of all human ills whether organic, functional, nervous, mental, emotional, acute or chronic.

Hermas—An apostolic father of the early church. He was formerly a Jew who accepted Christ as Messiah and wrote about his visions and prophetic utterances.

Hesychasm movement—A movement that first appeared in Byzantium during the thirteenth century. The followers of this movement devoted themselves in silence to spiritual meditation and prayer, attempting to come as close to God as they could.

Hilary of Poitiers (315–368)—A bishop of Poitiers, a great theologian and father of the early church. He also became one of the main defenders of the Orthodox view of the Godhead as pertaining to the trinity.

Hippolytus (died 236)—A presbyter and teacher for the church in Rome. His studies on the Book of Revelation and the Book of Daniel are noted works.

Huss, John (1373–1415)—A Bohemian reformer and martyr for the cause of Christ.

Hysteria—The same, in the religious sense, as emotionalism.

Ignatius (d. 107)—An apostolic father of the early church. He was taught by the apostles. His works are still in existence and reveal the thinking in the earliest time of the church. He was a bishop and an early martyr.

Imperative—The mood of volition (including command, request, strong request, strong desire, earnest desire, urgent desire, beseeching and entreaty) used to express the appeal of will to will, and due to that expresses plausibility in its weakest form.

Irenæus of Lyons (130–202)—A theologian and father of the early church. In his youth he was strongly influenced by St. Polycarp. His greatest work was that on heresies.

Isidore (560–636)—A theologian and father of the early church.

Jansenists—A radical Augustinian movement within the Roman Catholic Church during the seventeenth century.

Jerome of Prague (1371–1416)—A Bohemian reformer, a brilliant orator and debater, and a close friend of John Huss.

John of Damascus (673–749)—A Greek theologian and the very last of the Eastern fathers.

John the Monk—A Christian whom Augustine speaks of as having the gift of prophecy, besides other gifts.

Joseph of Arimathæa—A great member of the Jewish court of the Sanhedrin who had compassion for Jesus. (See Matthew 27:57–59; Mark 15:43; Luke 23:50.)

Liberalism—A system of politics, religion and society that supports and defends the idea of man being the center of the universe, man's final evolution to godhead, the idea of atheism, and the hatred for what the Holy Bible and Christianity stand for.

Luther, Martin (1463–1546)—A reformer, founder of Lutheranism and one who sparked the Great Reformation by writing his *Ninety-Five Theses*.

M.

Marcion—The chief opponent of Tertullian and a prominent heretic. He was the head of a form of gnosticism known as Asiatic gnosticism in the third century.

Martin of Tours, Saint (335–400)—The founder and the originator of monasticism in Gaul.

Martyr, Justin (100–165)—An early Christian apologist and father of the early church. His greatest work was in defending Christianity against Judaism. He fought against those who wanted Christianity and Judaism to be mixed into one religion.

Melito (second century)—An apostolic father of the early church and bishop of Sardis.

Methodius of Olympus (d. 311)—An ecclesiastical writer, bishop of Olympus and Lycia. He died a martyr.

Millennial kingdom—The earthly kingdom of Jesus Christ that is promised in the Old Testament prophecies to last one thousand years.

Millennium—The millennium is when Jesus Christ as the Son of David will reign over the millennial kingdom, fulfilling the prophecies in the Old Testament about an earthly kingdom in which the Messiah will reign. (See 2 Samuel 7; Psalms 2; 89:35–37; Isaiah 2:2–4; Daniel 2:44–45; 7:13–14; Zechariah 6:12–13.)

Miracles—Powers that mean explosions of almightiness.

Mnason of Cyprus—A friend of Paul and one of the earliest members of the Christian community. (See Acts 21:16.)

Modernism—Similar to secularism, but deals with materialism and the promotion of all that is material, like money, property and wealth.

Momentary future tense—Action in its entirety as instantaneous or timeless.

Montanism—A sect of Christianity that functioned from the second century to the ninth century whose founder was Montanus. For some time, Montanism was orthodox in all aspects, but was eventually heretical.

Moody, Dwight L. (1837–1899)—An American evangelist and theologian. At first, he became a Unitarian and then converted to Congregationalism. His first work for the Lord was in missionary work in Chicago. Later he became the pastor of Chicago Avenue Church, which after his death became the Moody Memorial Church.

Neo-Pentecostal circles—A new wave of Pentecostalism that has rejected, in many cases, the precautions of other Pentecostals throughout the centuries.

Neuter gender—It deals with those things or persons without sexual gender (not being either masculine or feminine).

O

Origen (185–254)—An Alexandrian biblical critic, theologian, father and ecclesiastical writer of the early church.

P

Passive voice—It is that which shows the subject as receiving some kind of action or as being the object of some kind of action.

Pentecost—The idea of Pentecost is the gifts of the Spirit and their manifestations, including tongues, healings, miracles, and other such manifestations.

Perfect state—It is a state of perfection, sinlessness, perfect peace and perfect harmony without any evil creature or any will not in conformity to God's will. It takes place after the millennium, after the last rebellion, after the Great White Throne Judgment, and when the heavens and the earth are made perfect.

Present tense—The idea of continuous, progressive or repetitive action in the present time.

Q

Quakers—A religious sect that received this name due to the trembling they sometimes experienced during their religious meetings. Quakers, as a sect, have been called the Society of Friends. It traces its origin back to the radical wing of English Puritanism of the 1640s.

R

Rapture—The glorious catching away of all true believers in Christ to meet the Lord in the air with those dead saints coming with Christ to be resurrected. In other words, it is the coming of the Lord for His saints, not the coming of the Lord with His saints.

Reformation—A term that deals with the revival, movement and revolution that truly began in the 1500s and continued to the 1700s. It began with Martin Luther.

Reformers—Those men or women who sought reform for the church. It deals almost exclusively with the time between the fourteenth century and the seventeenth century.

Resurrection—The process whereby the bodies of the dead are united with the souls of the dead, and the bodies are changed from corruption to incorruption and from mortality to immortality. In other words, the resurrection is the process whereby the souls of the dead will be restored to a bodily life without corruption in immortality.

Revivalists—Those men or women who were used by God to spark the massive revivals throughout the modern times, like John Wesley, Whitefield and others.

Rothwell—A great preacher and revivalist during the seventeenth century.

$$S$$

Samaritans—The inhabitants of Samaria.

Second Advent or the Second Coming—The glorious, literal, bodily and personal return of the Lord with His saints and angels to defeat the Dragon, the False Prophet, the Antichrist and his armies. His purpose is to deliver Israel, establish a reign of righteousness and holiness upon the earth, assist in fulfilling the mystery mentioned in Revelation 10:6–7 and begin the process of putting down all rebellion against God. (See 1 Corinthians 15:25–28.)

Secularism—A system of doctrines, beliefs, thoughts, ideas and practices that reject all forms of religion, especially Christianity, as useful.

Shakers—An American religious sect that arose in the eighteenth century in England. It supported the prophetic spirit of the early church. By 1706, there were two hundred to three hundred prophets in London alone. They stressed the approach of God's kingdom and the millennial state. In 1774 the first Shaker appeared in America.

Signs and wonders—Signs are the visible tokens of an invisible power while wonders are a staggering astonishment.

Subjunctive mood—In its original and simplest use, it expresses simple futurity, except that the futurity in view is not certain but conditional. Because of this, the subjunctive mood is known as the mood of objective plausibility, which is the same as probability, and is one step from reality, actuality and certainty. While the indicative, outside of the potential indicative, assumes reality, the subjunctive mood assumes unreality that could become reality under certain conditions.

Sulpit(c)ius Severus (360–420)—An apostle of Austria, historian, hagiographer, and father of the early church.

Tertullian (160–225)—An African church father, great theologian and great organizer of Christian doctrine.

Theodoric—The bishop of Croatia who lived about the time when Huss and Jerome were martyred.

Waldensians—A sect of Christianity that arose between the eleventh and twelfth centuries and continued throughout most of the nineteenth century. The Waldensian movement has been known as the First Reformation.

Weselus—A Franciscan who lived during the sixteenth century.

Wesley, John (1703–1791)—A revivalist, theologian and founder of Methodism.

Whitefield—A companion and contemporary of John Wesley.

INDEX

A

B

C

M

N

O

P

Q

Quakers: 51, 91

R

rapture: 3, 12, 62, 91
reception of the Holy Spirit: 41
Recognitions of Clement: 73
Reformation: 32–34, 64, 87, 89, 91, 93
reformers: 32–33, 92
resurrection: 3, 42, 49, 57, 73, 92
revivalists: *ix–x*, 32, 92
Rothwell: 75, 92

S

Saint Antony: 47
Saint Martin of Tours: 49
Samaritans: 25, 48, 92
Satan: 5, 8, 16, 18, 26–27, 49, 53–54, 58, 63, 84, 86
Satanists: *vii*
Second Advent: 3, 92
secularism: 32, 90, 92
Shakers: 51, 92
shaking: 51, 57, 64, 67–68, 72
slain in the Spirit: *ix–x*, 55, 60–61, 63–65, 67–68, 71, 73–74
sola Scriptura: 1
Stephen: 10, 20, 22
subjunctive mood: 3–4, 15, 92–93
Sulpit(c)ius Severus: 49

T

temporary: 1–2
Tertullian: 5, 36–38, 43, 62, 71
Theodoric: 34, 93
Thessalonians: 9
Timothy: 19, 20, 25
tongues: *xi*, 2–7, 26, 38, 45, 48, 51–52, 55, 57, 61, 65
tradition: 1, 26, 28, 35, 38, 56
trembling and quaking: *x*, 61, 63–65, 69, 74
Trophimus: 19–20

$\mathcal{W}$

For more information concerning Dr. Roberts, his mother, their schedule of events, their ministry and donations to that ministry, please contact:

True Light Ministries
P.O. Box 28538
Jacksonville, FL 32218
A Non-Profit and Tax-Exempt Organization
Cell: 904-472-7786
Fax: 904-751-0304
truelightministries.org

For I shall bring forth
truth out of darkness
for the sake of my people.